RAND NATIONAL SECURITY RESEARCH DIVISION

T0288562

Geographic and Demographic Representativeness of Junior Reserve Officer Training Corps

CHARLES A. GOLDMAN
JONATHAN SCHWEIG
MAYA BUENAVENTURA
CAMERON WRIGHT

For more information on this publication, visit www.rand.org/t/RR1712

Library of Congress Control Number: 2017950423

ISBN: 978-0-8330-9785-9

Published by the RAND Corporation, Santa Monica, Calif.

© Copyright 2017 RAND Corporation

RAND® is a registered trademark.

Cover imagess clockwise from top left: U.S Air Force photo, U.S. Navy photo, MCJROTC, Vickey Mouzé, U.S. Army Cadet Command Public Affairs

Support RAND

Make a tax-deductible charitable contribution at

www.rand.org/giving/contribute

www.rand.org

Preface

The Junior Reserve Officers' Training Corps (JROTC) is the largest youth training and development program in the United States, with more than 500,000 participating students. All five service branches maintain JROTC programs, which are operated through cooperative agreements between the services and high schools. The program includes classes covering such topics as leadership, civics, U.S. history, geography and global awareness, health and wellness, and life skills. The program also includes extracurricular activities, such as drill teams, color guards, orienteering, cybersecurity teams, and rifle teams.

Recently, there has been congressional interest in the representativeness of JROTC units. This report responds to these interests and motivations by exploring the representativeness of JROTC units in terms of geographic area (with a special focus on rural areas) and demographics (including race, ethnicity, and income) at the school level. This report also explores the laws and policies that affect the expansion of JROTC and the potential for the similar (but not federally funded) National Defense Cadet Corps to expand participation opportunities within current resource constraints. This report also offers suggestions for policies and practices that may promote or improve representativeness.

Although this report grew out of congressional interest in the representativeness of JROTC units, the findings and policy recommendations pertain to a wide audience, including JROTC service headquarters, JROTC regional directors, JROTC instructors, high school and school district administrators, policymakers, and the interested public.

This research was sponsored by the Office of the Secretary of Defense, Accession Policy, and conducted within the Forces and Resources Policy Center of the RAND National Defense Research Institute, a federally funded research and development center sponsored by the Office of the Secretary of Defense, the Joint Staff, the Unified Combatant Commands, the Department of the Navy, the Marine Corps, the defense agencies, and the defense Intelligence Community. For more information on the RAND Forces and Resources Policy Center, see www.rand.org/nsrd/ndri/centers/frp or contact the director (contact information is provided on the web page).

Contents

Preface iii
Figures and Tables vii
Summary ix
Acknowledgments xxi

CHAPTER ONE
Introduction 1
Key Features of the JROTC Program 3
NDCC 5
Study Objectives and Approach 6
Organization of This Report 8

CHAPTER TWO
Benefits of JROTC 11
Academic Benefits 11
Nonacademic Benefits 13

CHAPTER THREE
The Representativeness of JROTC 15
JROTC Is Underrepresented in About Two-Thirds of States 16
JROTC Is Underrepresented in Rural Areas 20
JROTC Programs Are Most Prevalent Among Medium and Large
    Schools and Underrepresented in Small Schools 23
JROTC Is Strongly Represented Among Schools Serving
    Economically Disadvantaged Populations 24
JROTC Is Well Represented at Schools Serving Minority
    Populations 26

Patterns in Representativeness May Reflect Prior Policy and Instructor
  Availability... 27
At the School Level, Female Cadets Are Slightly Underrepresented....... 28
Summary...29

CHAPTER FOUR
Factors That Affect the Initiation and Viability of JROTC Units 31
Service Policies and Initiatives Affect Three of the Factors.................33
Seven Factors Play Unique Roles in Starting and Maintaining JROTC
  Programs in Rural Areas, Underrepresented States, and
  Economically Disadvantaged Schools.................................... 38

CHAPTER FIVE
Recommendations.. 43
Use Program Alternatives, Such as NDCC, to Support Expansion in
  Rural Areas and Underrepresented States...................... ...., 44
Raise Awareness of JROTC Programs to Increase Geographic
  Representativeness 45
Consider Flexibility in Instructor Requirements for Rural Areas and
  Small Schools 46
Weigh the Benefits and Drawbacks of Changing Instructor-Salary
  Policy...47
Consider Changing and Standardizing Program Selection Criteria....... 48
Provide Remote Rural Schools with More Discretion in Allocating
  Travel Funding 48
Maintain Standardized Program Data That Can Be Easily Linked
  with External Data Sources 49
Consider Dedicated Funding for JROTC...................................49

CHAPTER SIX
Conclusion 51

APPENDIXES
A. Literature Review 55
B. Study Methods 67
C. JROTC Unit Distribution, by State and Service 77

Abbreviations...81
References 85

Figures and Tables

Figures

1.1. Distribution of JROTC Unit Sponsorship, April 2016 3
3.1. JROTC Program Prevalence Across U.S. States, 2015 17
3.2. Percentage of Public High Schools with JROTC Programs, by Census Division, 2015 18
3.3. Percentage of JROTC Units Sponsored by the Army Across U.S. States, 2015 21
3.4. Percentage of JROTC Units Sponsored by the Air Force Across U.S. States, 2015 21
3.5. Percentage of JROTC Units Sponsored by the Navy Across U.S. States, 2015 22
3.6. Percentage of JROTC Units Sponsored by the Marine Corps Across U.S. States, 2015 22
3.7. Percentage of Public High Schools with JROTC Programs, by Urbanicity, 2015 23
3.8. Percentage of High Schools with JROTC Programs, by Enrollment, 2015 24
3.9. Percentage of Public High Schools with JROTC Programs, by Title I Eligibility, 2015 25
4.1. Three Factors Affected by Service Policies and Initiatives 33

Tables

1.1. NDCC Units Sponsored by the Army, Air Force, Navy, and Marine Corps, April 2016 6
2.1. Studies That Examine the Association Between JROTC Participation and Academic and Nonacademic Outcomes 12

3.1.   Percentage of Students in NCES Race/Ethnicity Categories
       for Public High Schools with JROTC, Public High
       Schools Without JROTC, and All Public High Schools,
       2015.. 26
4.1.   School Candidate Ranking Factors for the Army, Air
       Force, Navy, and Marine Corps, 2015 37
4.2.   JROTC Challenges and Opportunities in Rural Areas 39
4.3.   JROTC Challenges and Opportunities in
       Underrepresented States.. 40
4.4.   JROTC Challenges and Opportunities in Economically
       Disadvantaged Schools 41
5.1.   Current JROTC Units, Planned JROTC Units, and
       Reasons for Recent Closures, April 2016 44

Summary

The Junior Reserve Officers' Training Corps (JROTC) was established in 1916 as a part of the National Defense Act as a leadership and citizenship program for students enrolled in secondary schools. All five service branches operate JROTC units, and these units served approximately 553,260 cadets in the United States and abroad during the 2015–2016 school year. As of April 2016, there were 3,390 JROTC units at U.S. high schools. The services spent about $370 million per year on JROTC, which is the equivalent of approximately $670 per cadet.

JROTC units are administered cooperatively by the services and the high schools. Specifically, the military services subsidize instructor salaries, the cost of uniforms, equipment, curricular materials (including textbooks), and some travel costs necessary for participation in cocurricular activities (including drill competitions and academic bowls). Schools agree to contribute to salaries, provide facilities for the program, and schedule times for JROTC programming. Although there is some variation across services, the JROTC curriculum typically includes up to four years of coursework in leadership, civics, U.S. history, geography and global awareness, health and wellness, and life skills.

All JROTC units have a minimum of two instructors. Unless there are extenuating circumstances, senior instructors are retired active-duty officers, and junior instructors are retired noncommissioned officers (NCOs). All services also allow retirement-eligible reservists and guard members to be certified as JROTC instructors. Each service certifies retired active-duty and reserve military personnel to be eligible to serve as JROTC instructors. Instructors are hired from this pool of certified personnel by the school districts and are civilian employees of the school. Schools with substantially more than 100 cadets enrolled may be authorized to hire more than two instructors.

Until 2001, there were statutory limitations that placed a cap on the number of operating JROTC units. While this cap has been lifted, the number of units operated by the services is currently constrained by budget allocations. All of the services essentially operate the maximum number of programs possible with available funding from the U.S. Department of Defense, limiting the potential for program expansion into schools with an interest in establishing a JROTC unit. In fact, each service currently maintains a waiting list of schools desiring new units, so that when units are closed (for example, for failing to maintain minimum enrollment), new JROTC units can be established. JROTC programs are widely distributed. High schools in all 50 states operate JROTC units, and there are units in four U.S. territories, the District of Columbia, and Department of Defense Education Activity schools overseas.

This report responds to recent congressional interest in whether the schools participating in JROTC programs are representative with respect to geographic area, with a special focus on whether rural areas are adequately represented. Specifically, Congress has raised concerns about the impact that closure policies may have on representation. Because unit selection and closure are interrelated (e.g., new school sites can be selected only when existing units close), we consider both selection and closure policies. Representativeness is an important issue for two reasons. First, the JROTC program is a publicly funded citizenship program, and it is important to ensure that there is equitable access to such a program in all areas of the country. Second, while the JROTC program is not a recruitment program, and recruitment is not stated among the program objectives, Congress has noted that the representativeness of the JROTC program is an important issue because of the implications for recruitment. Access to the JROTC program in all areas of the country helps to ensure that the services are able to recruit individuals from diverse backgrounds.

To respond to these interests and motivations, this report has two primary objectives. The first objective is to examine the representativeness of JROTC at the school level with respect to demographics and geographic area. We explore the distribution of JROTC units across demographic and geographic categories and describe the representativeness of the schools operating JROTC programs in each of those categories. For the purposes of this analysis, we examine representativeness by comparing the prevalence of JROTC units across categories. For example, if 10 percent of the public high schools in the United States had JROTC units, then we would describe the distribution of JROTC as representative at the state level if each state had JROTC programs operating in 10 percent of its high schools. However, if a state had much larger proportion of schools with JROTC units (e.g., 30 percent or 50 percent), we would consider JROTC to be overrepresented in that particular state. A benefit of defining representativeness in this way is that it is relatively easy to discern patterns of representativeness by visual inspection. We collected information on representativeness by merging JROTC program data with data on all public high schools in the United States from the Common Core of Data program of the National Center for Education Statistics (NCES).

The second objective is to explore and describe how federal law, service policy, and school and community factors affect a school's capacity to start and successfully sustain JROTC units. We reviewed policy documents and interviewed a geographically diverse set of service and school representatives—including 14 regional directors, four service headquarters, and nine high school principals and school district officials—regarding JROTC benefits and the challenges of unit administration.

Findings

We find that JROTC has been more successful in addressing demographic representativeness than it has been in addressing geographic representativeness. We also find that several factors affect a school's ability to start and sustain a unit and that three of these factors in particular—school and community awareness, instructor availability, and selection and closure—can be shaped and directly addressed through changes to service policy.

JROTC Has Strong Representation Among Schools with Demographically Diverse Populations

Compared with public high schools overall, JROTC is well represented among public high schools with larger-than-average minority populations. In general, schools operating JROTC programs have higher-than-average representation for minority students and lower-than-average representation for white students.

There is also evidence that JROTC is strongly represented in schools serving economically disadvantaged populations, whether measured by Title I eligibility or free and reduced-price lunch program participation.

JROTC Is Underrepresented in Rural Areas and in About Two-Thirds of States

There is at least one JROTC program in each of the 50 states. However, JROTC programs are far more prevalent in some areas of the country than in others, with a particular concentration in the Southeast. Between 40 and 65 percent of public high schools in Louisiana, Florida, Georgia, North Carolina, and South Carolina have JROTC programs. JROTC programs are least prevalent in the mountain states and parts of the Midwest. Less than 5 percent of public schools in many of these states have JROTC programs. These disparities suggest real differences in the prevalence of JROTC across states and do not merely reflect differences in the distribution of high schools or the number of students across states.

Urban areas (and particularly large and midsize cities) have high representation compared with rural areas, particularly rural areas that are farthest from urbanized areas and urban clusters. Approximately one out of every four public high schools in urbanized areas has a JROTC unit. In rural areas, this number is closer to one in 20. School size is at least a partial explanation for these differences. Rural areas have smaller high schools, and smaller high schools are less likely to host JROTC units.

Several Factors Affect Starting and Sustaining Units

To address the report's second objective and describe how federal law, service policy, and school and community factors affect a school's capacity to start and successfully sustain JROTC units, we created, through a literature review and interviews, a conceptual model to describe the factors that influence the creation and sustainment of JROTC units. We identified seven such factors: (1) school and community awareness, (2) community support, (3) school facilities, (4) instructor availability, (5) student participation, (6) funding, and (7) selection and closures.

While all seven factors are important in understanding the creation and sustainment of JROTC units, we find that services' policies and initiatives are most likely to affect three of the factors: (1) school and community awareness, (2) instructor availability, and (3) selection and closures. Community support and student participation are less likely to be affected by service policy and initiatives because they are often tied to preexisting military sentiment within the community. Services do not have funds to build classrooms, storage facilities, and drill areas for schools that wish to initiate JROTC programs. Beyond their financial support of instructor salaries and operating costs, the services are unlikely to affect funding because services and school districts must operate within their respective budgetary constraints.

It is also worth noting that low growth and turnover of units limit opportunities to address representativeness. Specifically, this study was conducted at a time when budget constraints faced by the individual services had resulted in caps on the total number of JROTC programs that could be operated and maintained. All services currently operate at these caps, and, therefore, there is no room to increase representativeness by adding additional programs under these constraints. This issue is compounded because there is little turnover in JROTC programs. Given the essentially stable number of programs, changes occur largely through closures and openings of units at a limited number of schools on the school candidate lists, which are ranked lists of schools that have expressed interest in opening JROTC units, maintained by each service. Representativeness will be affected only gradually by these small changes in program distribution. This means that policy options to promote JROTC representation in underrepresented states and rural areas are limited.

Recommendations

This report explores the representativeness of JROTC programs and the factors that affect a school's capacity to start and successfully sustain JROTC units. Based on our findings, we recommend eight potential actions that could help to promote representativeness, particularly in rural areas.

Explore Program Alternatives to Support Expansion in Rural Areas and Underrepresented States

Because of budget constraints, services are unable to offer JROTC programs to all schools that are interested in establishing units. The National Defense Cadet Corps (NDCC) allows schools that are able to finance fully the instructor salaries and other program costs to offer an alternative program that is similar in many ways to the JROTC program in content and structure. For example, the services report that NDCC programs follow JROTC standards and use the same curriculum materials. The key difference is the program funding. The services provide materials and instructor training to NDCC units in the same manner as JROTC units, but schools must pay all other costs. As of April 2016, there were 111 NDCC units at U.S. high schools. Expansion of the NDCC program may offer schools in underrepresented areas an opportunity to offer JROTC-like programs, albeit without the financial support offered to JROTC units. NDCCs could be used to make room for new JROTC units within the existing unit caps. NDCC can also be used as a soft landing for underenrolled units. These underenrolled units could avoid closure by transferring to NDCC and would make room for the establishment of new JROTC units. These new units could then be concentrated in underrepresented states and rural areas. In short, NDCCs can promote expansion of JROTC into geographically underrepresented areas by generating more turnover.

NDCCs could also be promoted as an option for communities with the ability to fully fund units. By expanding NDCC in underrepresented areas with the ability to fully fund units, NDCC offers the opportunity to build awareness and community support in underrepresented areas without the costs of opening JROTC units in these areas. In addition, these NDCC units established in rural areas and underrepresented states could eventually be transitioned to JROTC units, if desired, when units become available.

Raise Awareness of JROTC Programs to Increase Geographic Representativeness

Our research suggests that there is a strong network effect in the development of JROTC programs: Schools and school districts learn about the program and its benefits from other schools in their local areas. However, rural schools tend to be more isolated, and states with low JROTC representation might have only weak networks. Because of this, it might be more important for the services to focus marketing and outreach resources to raise awareness of JROTC programs in these geographic areas. The services have marketed JROTC to underrepresented areas by visiting schools in underrepresented states to network with school districts and by sending letters to school districts throughout the United States. The Air Force recently opened new units in Idaho and Montana after visiting schools in these states and networking with school districts. When it instituted its NDCC program in 2011, the Navy sent a letter to every school district in the United States to raise awareness. If manpower and resources are available, the services could increase similar marketing and outreach in rural areas and underrepresented states.

Our research also suggests that rural areas may have difficulty in attracting potential instructors. A marketing and outreach effort could be made with respect to potential JROTC instructors, a key component of successful JROTC units. These marketing and outreach efforts would be directed toward military retirees in underrepresented states and rural areas to increase instructor pools in these areas.

Consider Flexibility in Instructor Requirements for Rural Areas and Small Schools

Our research suggests that high-quality instructors are critical to program success. Rural areas in particular may have difficulty in attracting potential instructors that meet the current requirements outlined by the services. While the services use waivers to allow NCOs in regions where senior-instructor positions are hard to fill, waiver processes vary considerably across the services. Formalizing processes for hiring well-qualified NCOs with bachelor's degrees for senior-instructor positions could expand the pool of instructors for underrepresented states, rural areas, and low-income areas. For small schools, the services might also consider alternatives to the traditional model of two full-time JROTC instructors.

Provide Remote Rural Schools with More Discretion in Allocating Travel Funding

Our research suggests that a school's capacity to start and successfully sustain a JROTC unit is related to levels of student participation and that successful JROTC units provide ample opportunities for leadership, extracurricular activities, and competitions. The cost of traveling to competitions and other extracurricular events is relatively higher for units in remote, rural areas because units may be as far as 100 miles from the next-closest unit. Distribution of travel funds to units varies by service. Providing regional directors with discretion in distributing funds may allow them to assist remote, rural schools that must travel longer distances to participate in competitions and extracurricular activities.

Carefully Weigh the Benefits and Drawbacks of Changing Instructor-Salary Policy

The services should carefully weigh the benefits and drawbacks of changing instructor-salary policy. Some services recently reduced instructor-salary support to ten months instead of 12. If the services adopted this policy for all instructors, cost savings could potentially permit the establishment of new JROTC units by reducing the cost per unit. However, some service representatives note that the adoption of ten-month instructor contracts may affect instructor interest in JROTC in general and may particularly affect interest in hard-to-fill locations.

Consider Changing and Standardizing Program Selection Criteria

The services and the Office of the Secretary of Defense may want to consider a more standardized approach to selection criteria, with uniform weighting on key factors that affect demographic representativeness (e.g., Title I eligibility, indicators of need, share of racial and ethnic minorities) and geographic representation (e.g., state representation, rural versus metropolitan area).

However, in formulating this approach, it is important to balance the goals of representativeness and program success. Some scoring criteria on school candidate lists may make it harder for schools in rural areas to rank highly, but these criteria are associated with program success. For example, school size is important for maintaining minimum enrollment requirements, and instructor-management factors, such as quality of life and proximity to a metropolitan area, make the retention of quality instructors possible. However, these factors may also weigh against rural schools and underrepresented states. While changing selection criteria might benefit geographically underrepresented areas, these changes could raise risks to program sustainability.

In short, services should consider adopting uniform weights for factors that promote optimal demographic representativeness and geographic representation. However, in determining the relative values of these weights, services should consider trade-offs such as quality of life for instructors.

Maintain Standardized Program Data That Can Be Easily Linked with External Data Sources

We recommend that the services continue to maintain consistent, timely, and comparable program data, using formats to be agreed on among the services and the Office of the Secretary of Defense. We also recommend that the services add NCES school identification numbers to JROTC program data to ease future analysis of demographic and geographic representativeness. All public U.S. high schools are assigned stable, unique identification numbers by NCES. These numbers allow the Common Core of Data to be linked with other sources. Currently, JROTC program data maintained by the services do not contain NCES identification numbers. To facilitate future analysis, including analyses of demographic and geographic representativeness, we recommend that the services add NCES identification numbers to their program data.

Consider Dedicated Funding for JROTC

Congress has expressed an interest in increasing the number of JROTC units, but the services have been constrained by their budgets. If Congress desires expansion of JROTC, Congress should consider appropriating funds dedicated to JROTC. Currently, any additional funding appropriated to the services and any savings realized through JROTC service initiatives (such as adopting ten-month instructor contracts) do not have to be invested in JROTC. If dedicated funding is provided and if JROTC expansions are targeted to underrepresented states and rural areas that can sustain successful programs, representation in these states and areas will increase.

Conclusion

Our study investigated the extent to which schools operating JROTC units are representative of the population of public schools in the country as a whole, both in terms of school demographics and geography, and explored how federal law, service policy, and local factors affect a school's capacity to start and sustain JROTC units. The results of our analysis of geographic and demographic representativeness suggest that JROTC policy and initiatives have been more successful in addressing some kinds of representation than others. Compared with public high schools overall, JROTC is well represented among public high schools with larger-than-average minority populations. In general, schools operating JROTC programs have higher-than-average representation for minority students and lower-than-average representation for white students. There is also evidence that JROTC is strongly represented in schools serving economically disadvantaged populations, whether measured by Title I eligibility or by participation in a free and reduced-price lunch program. However, JROTC is underrepresented in about two-thirds of states and in rural areas.

The results of our analysis of the factors that influence JROTC program start-up and sustainability indicate that many factors are likely outside the control of the services, and individual services face budget constraints that cap the total number of JROTC programs that can be operated and maintained. With these constraints in mind, we recommend eight potential actions to positively affect school and community awareness, instructor availability, and selection and closures. Congress should consider appropriating funds dedicated to JROTC to increase the number of JROTC units.

Acknowledgments

Individuals from the Junior Reserve Officers' Training Corps (JROTC), the U.S. Department of Defense, and school districts across the United States contributed to this work. Our conversations with these individuals greatly improved our understanding of the administration and implementation of JROTC at all levels. We especially wish to thank the principals and JROTC instructors at the high schools we visited for graciously arranging our visits, opening their classrooms and facilities to us, and speaking with us about their programs. Our understanding of JROTC was greatly enriched by these site visits.

We would like to thank the many Department of Defense officials who assisted us and provided feedback as we conducted the study. From the Office of the Secretary of Defense Accession Policy, we thank Christopher Arendt, Dennis Drogo, Gail Lovisone, and Stephanie Miller. From the military services, we thank Lydia Bethea, Carmen Cole, Timothy Dasseler, Peter Gray, Jennifer Hubal, Scott Lewis, Leon McMullen, Jeffrey Rosa, J. D. Smith, Linden St. Clair, Mark Watson, and Bobby Woods, as well as numerous others on their staffs.

We also thank RAND colleagues Craig Bond, Curtis Gilroy, Lisa Harrington, and Nelson Lim for their careful reviews and help in improving this report.

CHAPTER ONE

Introduction

The Junior Reserve Officers' Training Corps (JROTC) was established in 1916 as a part of the National Defense Act as a leadership and citizenship program for students enrolled in secondary schools (Public Law 64-85, 1916). According to its mission statement in Section 2031 of United States Code, Title 10 (2012), JROTC's purpose is "to instill in students in United States secondary educational institutions the value of citizenship, service to the United States, personal responsibility, and a sense of accomplishment." JROTC is designed to develop positive personal characteristics; create a sense of belonging; and foster interest in serving the community, staying in school, and attending college.[1]

From 1916 until the 1960s, only the Army sponsored JROTC units. In the 1919–1920 academic year, approximately 45,000 students participated in Army JROTC (Center for Strategic and International Studies, 1999). Enrollment increased to approximately 72,000 by 1942 (Center for Strategic and International Studies, 1999). In 1964, Public Law 88-647, the Reserve Officers' Training Corps Vitalization Act, directed the Air Force, the Navy, and the Marine Corps to establish JROTC units. In 1976, Public Law 94-361 increased the total autho-

---

[1] School principals and service representatives noted these goals during our interviews. In addition, in a survey conducted by Crawford, Thomas, and Estrada (2004), JROTC instructors' rank-ordered goals were (1) developing character and values, (2) developing citizenship, (3) developing leadership, (4) keeping students in school, (5) creating a sense of belonging, (6) teaching life skills, (7) creating openness in life opportunities, (8) improving academic performance, (9) creating interest in college, and (10) creating interest in the military.

rized number of JROTC units from 1,200 to 1,600. The 1993 National Defense Authorization Act (Public Law 102-484, 1992) again raised the maximum number of JROTC units, from 1,600 to 3,500 (Center for Strategic and International Studies, 1999). General Colin Powell initiated this expansion of JROTC in the 1990s in the wake of 1992 Los Angeles riots. Powell believed that expansion of the program, especially in high schools in impoverished urban areas, could address the lack of opportunities for youth in these cities, an issue that was highlighted by the riots (Powell, 1995).

Congress has expressed an interest in increasing the number of JROTC units. For instance, the National Defense Authorization Act for Fiscal Year 2009 required the Secretary of Defense to develop a plan to establish and support 3,700 JROTC units by 2020 (Public Law 110-417, 2008). However, the services' budget constraints have prevented them from expanding to this desired level. As of April 2016, the services were about 300 units short of the goal: There were 3,390 JROTC units at U.S. high schools.

Figure 1.1 illustrates how unit sponsorship is distributed among the services.

The Army operates just over 50 percent of the JROTC units. The Air Force operates approximately one-quarter of all units, and the remaining one-quarter is composed of units operated by the Navy, Marine Corps, and Coast Guard.[2]

Today, demand for the programs exceeds the operational capacity (i.e., the maximum number of programs that can be administered at current funding levels), and each service maintains a waiting list of schools desiring new units (Corbett and Coumbe, 2001). Although special measures have been taken to try to increase participation among schools that serve at-risk youth (particularly, economically disadvantaged youth), geographic representativeness of participating institutions remains a key issue for JROTC. The remaining sections of this chapter provide background on the operational structure of JROTC

---

[2] Because the Coast Guard only has two JROTC units and no National Defense Cadet Corps (NDCC) units, our report focuses on the Army, the Air Force, the Marine Corps, and the Navy. When we refer to *services*, we are referring to these four services.

Figure 1.1
Distribution of JROTC Unit Sponsorship, April 2016

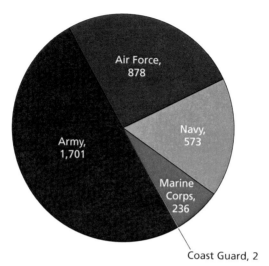

SOURCE: Service-provided program data as of April 2016.
RAND *RR1712-1.1*

and a brief description of the NDCC program, a JROTC-like program also operated by the services, as context for the current study.

Key Features of the JROTC Program

All five service branches operate JROTC units, and these units served approximately 553,000 cadets in the United States and abroad during the 2015–2016 school year. As of April 2016, there were 3,390 JROTC units at U.S. high schools. The services spent about $370 million per year on JROTC, which is the equivalent of approximately $670 per cadet.[3]

_____

[3] Data on the number of JROTC cadets in the United States and abroad, the number of JROTC units at U.S. high schools, and JROTC budgets were provided by the services in 2015 and 2016.

Each service has headquarters to administer the program and develop service-specific policy. JROTC programs are offered through partnerships between high schools and the military services. The military services subsidize instructor salaries, uniforms and other equipment, curricular materials (including textbooks), and some travel costs. Schools agree to contribute to salary, provide facilities for the program, and schedule times for JROTC programming. JROTC curriculum includes up to four years of coursework in leadership, civics, U.S. history, geography and global awareness, health and wellness, and life skills. High schools may offer core, elective, or physical education credits for JROTC participation. JROTC programs often include cocurricular and extracurricular activities in addition to the academic activities. These cocurricular and extracurricular activities include drill teams, color guards, orienteering, cybersecurity teams, rifle teams, and adventure training.[4]

After a school is selected for unit establishment, the sponsoring service and the school district enter into an agreement that governs the administration of the unit. In general, the agreements require that the school maintain JROTC enrollment of no fewer than 100 students who are in ninth grade or above (or, for schools with fewer than 1,000 students, 10 percent of the student enrollment); that the school provide adequate facilities for classroom instruction, drill, instructor offices, and extracurricular activities; and that the school employ a senior instructor and a junior instructor.

Unless there are extenuating circumstances, senior instructors are retired active-duty officers, and junior instructors are noncommissioned officers (NCOs). All services also allow retirement-eligible reservists and guard members to be certified as JROTC instructors. Each service certifies retired active-duty and reserve military personnel to be eligible to serve as JROTC instructors. Instructors are hired from this pool of certified personnel by the school districts and are civilian employees of the school. Schools with substantially more than 100 cadets enrolled may be authorized to hire more than two instructors.

---

[4] More-detailed information about curriculum scope and sequence, as well as service-specific extracurricular activities can be found on the services' JROTC websites.

When a senior-instructor position is hard to fill and has been vacant for an extended period, the services apply waivers to allow NCOs to fill the senior-instructor role ("NCO waiver").[5] There is some variation between the services in NCO waiver policies. For example, if the Air Force cannot fill a senior-instructor position for an extended period, the Air Force will contact the school to obtain the school's consent to use an NCO waiver for the position. If there is a hard-to-fill senior-instructor vacancy for a Marine JROTC unit, the school requests a waiver from the JROTC regional director to hire an NCO for the position.

NDCC

Because of budget constraints, the services are unable to offer JROTC programs to all schools that are interested in establishing units. NDCC allows schools that are able to finance fully the instructor salaries and other program costs to offer JROTC-like programs. The services provide curriculum materials and instructor training to NDCC units in the same manner as JROTC units, but schools must pay all other costs. As of April 2016, there were 111 NDCC units at U.S. high schools. The number of NDCC units sponsored by each service as of April 2016 is listed in Table 1.1.

As illustrated in Table 1.1, there are very few NDCC units overall, although this number has been growing, and the distribution of NDCC units among the services does not mirror the distribution of the JROTC units. For example, the Army operates less than one-third of the NDCC programs, but it operates more than one-half of the JROTC programs.

The services report that NDCC programs follow JROTC standards. All services except the Navy require schools to follow JROTC

---

[5] Department of Defense Instruction 1205.13 (2006), paragraph E2.2.2.1, provides: "Single JROTC units and each subunit of a multiple JROTC unit require one officer instructor and one enlisted instructor. When necessary, the Military Service concerned may authorize the substitution of officers for enlisted instructors, and conversely, may authorize the substitution of enlisted for officer instructors."

Table 1.1
NDCC Units Sponsored by the Army, Air
Force, Navy, and Marine Corps, April 2016

Service	Number of NDCC Units
Army	33
Air Force	14
Navy	38
Marine Corps	26
Total	111

SOURCE: Service-provided program data as of
April 2016.

instructor-salary guidelines. NDCC units are managed in the same
way as JROTC at the service-headquarters level for the Army, the
Air Force, the Marine Corps, and the Navy. One notable difference
between JROTC and NDCC policies is that the Navy and the Marine
Corps allow for a 50-cadet minimum and one rather than two instructors for their NDCC programs.

Study Objectives and Approach

JROTC programs are widely distributed. Programs operate in all 50
states, four U.S. territories, the District of Columbia, and Department of Defense Education Activity schools overseas. There has been
recent congressional interest in whether the schools participating in
JROTC programs are representative with respect to geographic area,
with a special focus on whether rural areas are adequately represented.
Specifically, Senate Report 113-211 (2014), accompanying H.R. 4870,
Department of Defense Appropriations Act, 2015, raises concerns
about the impact that closure policies may have on representation.
Because unit selection and closure are interrelated, we consider both
selection and closure policies.

There are several reasons why representativeness is important.
First, the JROTC program is a publicly funded citizenship program,

and it is important to ensure that there is equitable access to such a program in all areas of the country. Second, while the JROTC program is not a recruitment program, and recruitment is not stated among the program objectives, the Senate report notes that the representativeness of the JROTC programs is an important issue because of the implications for recruitment (Senate Report 113-211, 2014). Access to JROTC programs in all areas of the country helps to ensure that the services are able to recruit individuals from diverse backgrounds.

To respond to these interests and motivations, this report has two primary objectives. The first is to examine the representativeness of JROTC at the school level with respect to geography and demographics. We explore the distribution of JROTC units across demographic and geographic categories and describe the representativeness of the schools operating JROTC programs in each of those categories. For the purposes of this analysis, we examine representativeness by comparing the prevalence of JROTC units across categories. For example, if 10 percent of the public high schools in the United States had JROTC units, then we would describe the distribution of JROTC as representative at the state level if each state had JROTC programs operating in 10 percent of its high schools. However, if a state had much larger proportion of schools with JROTC units (e.g., 30 percent or 50 percent), we would consider JROTC to be overrepresented in that particular state. A benefit of defining representativeness in this way is that it is relatively easy to discern patterns of representativeness by visual inspection.

In this report, we examine school-level representativeness. School-level representativeness allows us to identify whether a student at a given school would have an opportunity to join JROTC because a unit exists at that school. To examine the geographic and demographic representativeness of JROTC, we needed data on (1) the location, demographics, high school affiliation, and service affiliation of each JROTC unit and (2) the location, demographics, and enrollment of all public high schools in the United States. JROTC program data were provided to us by the services and included location data for both JROTC and NDCC units. We used the Common Core of Data collected and housed by the National Center for Education Statistics (NCES), part of the U.S. Department of Education, as the source of information on U.S. high schools. This data source includes school-level geographic and demographic information about every public high school in the United States. Because NCES school identification numbers were not included in the data provided by the services, we used zip codes for initial matches and hand-checking to resolve ambiguities. Our final data set contains records for 21,227 public high schools (JROTC and non-JROTC). We found that JROTC has strong representation among schools with demographically diverse populations. As noted, Powell believed that expansion of JROTC could address the lack of opportunities for youth in urban areas (Powell, 1995). Thus, program objectives may weigh in favor of overrepresentation among demographic groups and in geographic regions that experience disadvantage.

The second objective is to determine how federal laws and policies affect starting and sustaining JROTC units, including policies for unit closure and selection. We also analyze factors that influence the feasibility of using NDCC programs as an option for schools that do not receive approval for a JROTC unit. We interviewed service and school representatives from a wide variety of geographic areas, including 14 regional directors, four service headquarters, and nine high school principals and school district officials. Interview topics included benefits of JROTC, challenges with JROTC unit administration, instructor hiring, and NDCC. We identify a number of factors that present challenges for improving representativeness. We offer several policy recommendations for addressing these factors, including the expansion of NDCC.

Organization of This Report

Chapter Two summarizes the literature on the benefits of JROTC program participation. Chapter Three describes insights we gained about geographic and demographic representativeness, and Chapter Four describes the insights we gained about the factors that may influence representativeness. Chapter Five provides policy recommendations on promoting greater representativeness. Chapter Six suggests some further steps for research and exploration. Appendix A provides a thorough literature review, Appendix B describes in detail the methods used to assess the representativeness of the JROTC programs and the methods used to explore the barriers and facilitators to successful program operation, and Appendix C lists the distribution of JROTC units by state and service.

CHAPTER TWO

Benefits of JROTC

In this chapter, we describe the benefits of participating in JROTC programs, drawing on the existing literature (as summarized in Appendix A) and project interviews. There is consensus in the existing literature that JROTC participation has both academic and nonacademic benefits for students (Table 2.1). We briefly describe these benefits and the evidence base for these claims.

Academic Benefits

Research on the associations between JROTC participation and academic outcomes is summarized in the first section of Table 2.1. Studies that examined academic outcomes found consistently positive associations between grade point average (GPA) and JROTC participation. JROTC participation was also consistently associated with lower dropout rates and improved attendance. The evidence on other academic benefits, including graduation rates and improved performance on standardized tests (including statewide assessments), showed mixed results.

A study of JROTC Career Academies that focused on at-risk youth and that statistically controlled for self-selection into the program also found an association between JROTC participation and increased GPAs, increased attendance rates, and increased graduation

Table 2.1
Studies That Examine the Association Between JROTC Participation and
Academic and Nonacademic Outcomes

| | Studies | | |
Student Outcome	Positive	No Statistically Significant Relationship	Total
Academic benefit			
GPA	2	0	2
Attendance rate	2	0	2
Standardized test score	3	3	6
Dropout rate	2	0	2
Graduation rate	4	1	5
Nonacademic benefit			
Discipline rate	1	0	1
Personal characteristic (e.g., leadership, self-esteem)	5	3	8
College enrollment rate	0	1	1
Military enlistment	3	1	4

SOURCES: Bachmann, 1994; Biggs, 2010; Bulach, 2002; Center for Strategic and International Studies (CSIS), 1999; Curran, 2007; Flowers, 1999; Hawkins, 1988; Pema and Mehay, 2009a; Pema and Mehay, 2009b; Seiverling, 1973; Roberts, 1991; William-Bonds, 2013.

NOTES: Most of the 12 studies examined more than one outcome. For graduation rates and personal characteristics, one of the studies (Pema and Mehay, 2009a) showed improvements for African American cadets only.

rates (Elliot, Hanser, and Gilroy, 2002).[1] Because Career Academies have a number of other intensive components, it is more difficult to determine whether these outcomes are associated with JROTC or

---

[1] JROTC Career Academies are a partnership between the U.S. Department of Defense (DoD), the U.S. Department of Education, individual school districts, and the business community. Career academies are schools within schools, which personalize instruction and provide leadership and vocational and academic training to youth at risk of dropping out of school.

other education and vocational components of Career Academies. For this reason, the study on student outcomes at Career Academies is not included among the studies in Table 2.1.

Nonacademic Benefits

The second section of Table 2.1 shows a summary of the associations between JROTC participation and nonacademic student outcomes. One study (CSIS, 1999) examined discipline rates and found a positive association between improved student outcomes and JROTC participation. In addition—while our interviewees noted that JROTC helps students develop good character, leadership skills, and positive relationships with adult role models—the literature on this topic has yielded mixed results. Some studies found a positive association between JROTC participation and personal characteristics, and others did not any find statistically significant associations.

The single study on college enrollment rates (Biggs, 2010) did not find a statistically significant difference between the enrollment rates of a sample of JROTC cadets at four high schools and a matched sample of students who did not participate in JROTC.

Other benefits of JROTC participation were mentioned frequently in interviews. According to high school principals and service representatives, JROTC provides a place for students who are not involved in athletics or school band to be part of a student community and to participate in extracurricular activities. These interviewees also noted that JROTC provides volunteer opportunities that allow students to benefit the larger community outside school.

In addition to improved academic and behavioral outcomes, services provide other benefits to cadets. Cadets are given specific opportunities to compete for ROTC college scholarships and service academy appointments, although these benefits are certainly not granted to all former JROTC cadets. JROTC cadets who choose to enlist in the military are allowed to start at E-2, one pay grade higher than most other enlistees, providing some additional income when they enlist.

Although JROTC is not designed for military recruitment, studies have examined the association between JROTC participation and military enlistment. Two studies (Pema and Mehay, 2009a; Biggs, 2010) found a positive correlation between JROTC and enlistment. One study found a positive correlation only for students who enrolled in JROTC early in high school and persisted in the program through senior year (Pema and Mehay, 2009b). Another study found that the impact of JROTC participation on military enlistment decisions is negligible when self-selection into the JROTC program is accounted for (Days and Ang, 2004). Three of these studies used nationwide surveys of high school students, with the exception of Biggs (2010), which used data from four high schools.

CHAPTER THREE

The Representativeness of JROTC

In this chapter, we discuss our findings regarding geographic and demographic representativeness. As detailed in Chapter One, we examined representativeness by comparing the prevalence of JROTC units across a variety of demographic and geographic categories. We explored geographic representativeness in two different ways: First, we explored state-level representation. Although all 50 states have at least one JROTC program, programs are not evenly distributed among the states. Thus, the first stage of our investigation was to explore representation across the states. Second, we explored representativeness in rural areas using the rural and urban classifications from the U.S. Census Bureau.

We explored several different aspects of demographic representativeness, including economic disadvantage, race and ethnicity, and gender. We also explored the relationship between school size and the presence of JROTC programs. We used two measures as proxies for economic disadvantage—Title I eligibility and free and reduced-price lunch eligibility. The Title I program was established in 1965 as a part of the Elementary and Secondary Education Act and allocates funding for schools and school districts serving students who come from low-income families or are otherwise disadvantaged (Public Law 89-10, 1965). Free and reduced-price lunch eligibility is commonly used as proxy for economic disadvantage, as many students who are eligible for this program live below the poverty threshold.

As a reminder, all of the analyses in this chapter (with the exception of gender) are at the school level. Therefore our conclusions about representativeness reflect on whether the schools operating JROTC are representative of school-level demographics—we are not able to make any inferences about the representativeness of programs within schools.

JROTC Is Underrepresented in About Two-Thirds of States

There is at least one JROTC program in each of the 50 states. However, as illustrated in Figure 3.1, these programs are not evenly distributed across the states. Shading on the map indicates the percentage of public high schools in each state that host JROTC programs: darker for higher percentages and lighter for lower percentages. If each state had equal representation, we would see that each state, overall, would be similarly shaded in Figure 3.1. However, this is not the case. JROTC programs are far more prevalent in some states than in others, with a particular concentration in the Southeast. Between 40 and 65 percent of public high schools in Louisiana, Florida, Georgia, North Carolina, and South Carolina have JROTC programs. JROTC programs are most sparse in the mountain states and parts of the Midwest. Less than 5 percent of public schools in many of these states have JROTC programs. Approximately 16 percent of public high schools in the United States have JROTC units, so states are underrepresented when less than 16 percent of their public high schools have JROTC units. Appendix C provides the map's data in tabular form, for reference.

This same pattern of representation can be seen when we look at patterns in representation by census division.[1] Figure 3.2 presents the

---

[1] Each of the four census regions is divided into two or more census divisions. The Northeast region is composed of

- the New England division: Connecticut, Maine, Massachusetts, New Hampshire, Rhode Island, and Vermont
- the Middle Atlantic division: New Jersey, New York, and Pennsylvania.

The Midwest region is composed of

- the East North Central division: Illinois, Indiana, Michigan, Ohio, and Wisconsin
- the West North Central division: Iowa, Kansas, Minnesota, Missouri, Nebraska, North Dakota, and South Dakota.

Figure 3.1
JROTC Program Prevalence Across U.S. States, 2015

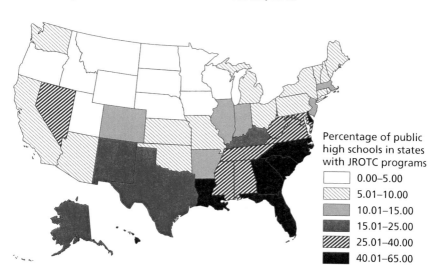

Percentage of public
high schools in states
with JROTC programs
- 0.00–5.00
- 5.01–10.00
- 10.01–15.00
- 15.01–25.00
- 25.01–40.00
- 40.01–65.00

SOURCE: Project calculations from JROTC program data provided by the services in 2015 and the NCES Common Core of Data from the 2012–2013 school year (NCES, undated-a).
RAND *RR1712-3.1*

percentage of public high schools in each of nine census divisions that operate JROTC programs.

If the programs were equally represented in all divisions, we would expect the bars in Figure 3.2 to be the same height. However, the bars for the South Atlantic, East South Central, and West South Central

---

The South region is composed of

- the South Atlantic division: Delaware, District of Columbia, Florida, Georgia, Maryland, North Carolina, South Carolina, Virginia, and West Virginia
- the East South Central division: Alabama, Kentucky, Mississippi, and Tennessee
- the West South Central division: Arkansas, Louisiana, Oklahoma, and Texas.

The West region is composed of

- the Mountain division: Arizona, Colorado, Idaho, Montana, Nevada, New Mexico, Utah, and Wyoming
- the Pacific division: Alaska, California, Hawaii, Oregon, and Washington.

Information on the census regions and divisions can be found in U.S. Census Bureau, 2015.

**Figure 3.2
Percentage of Public High Schools with JROTC Programs, by Census
Division, 2015**

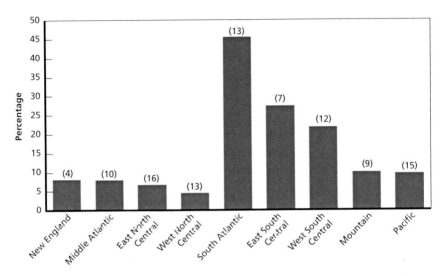

SOURCE: Project calculations from JROTC program data provided by the services in
2015 and the NCES Common Core of Data from the 2012–2013 school year (NCES,
undated-a).
NOTE: The number in parentheses indicates the percentage of all U.S. public high
schools in the census division.
RAND RR1712-3.2

divisions are significantly taller, suggesting overrepresentation in these
states. In the South Atlantic division, 45 percent of public high schools
have JROTC programs. Similarly, we see much shorter bars in several
divisions, including the West North Central and New England, where
only 5 percent and 8 percent, respectively, of public high schools have
JROTC programs.

These results are not sensitive to state or regional differences in the
number of schools or students served. Even when accounting for differences in the number of high schools in each state and school enrollment,
JROTC is overrepresented in the South Atlantic region—particularly in
Florida, Georgia, North Carolina, and South Carolina.

From a policy perspective for the services, given limited resources
and deep institutional knowledge about the factors that drive program

success, achieving representativeness in states or census areas that are sparsely populated might not be a priority, and generating awareness and interest in these areas presents particular challenges. In Chapter Four, we explore some of these factors and elaborate on these challenges in greater detail. However, there are geographic regions that have large populations that have lower JROTC representation. For example, the Pacific division (which includes California) serves nearly one-fifth of the country's high school students. But only about one-quarter of the region's students have access to JROTC (compared with nearly two-thirds in the South Atlantic). Efforts to increase JROTC representation in these areas would provide the relatively large population of high school students in these states with the opportunity to participate in JROTC.

Services Vary in Their Representation Across States

To explore factors that may be associated with the overall geographic distribution of JROTC units, we specifically examined the distribution of each service's units across states, which are illustrated in the choropleth maps in Figures 3.3 through 3.6 (complete data on the distribution of JROTC units by service and state are available in Appendix C). The percentage of JROTC units in each state that is sponsored by the relevant service is color-coded on each map. As in Figure 3.1, darker colors indicate higher concentrations, and lighter colors indicate lower concentrations. The numerator in the fraction that determines how each state is shaded is the number of units in that state sponsored by the relevant service, and the denominator is the total number of JROTC units in the state. For each service, the scale is centered on that service's average share of all JROTC units to display variations around the service's average rate. If we did not center the scales in this way, the maps would be largely unrevealing: the Army, with its large overall share of units, would have many dark states, while the Marine Corps, with its small share, would have mostly light states.

For example, Figure 3.3 illustrates the distribution of Army units. In Figure 3.3, Texas is colored a shade that indicates that 40 to 60 percent of the units are sponsored by the Army. In other words, of the total number of JROTC units in Texas, 40 to 60 percent of the units are sponsored by the Army.

As illustrated in Figure 3.3, the share of Army-sponsored units is fairly even across states. As illustrated in Figure 3.5, Navy units are concentrated in coastal states. As illustrated in Figures 3.4 and 3.6, Air Force and Marine units are concentrated in certain states, but no pattern is apparent upon visual inspection.

JROTC Is Underrepresented in Rural Areas

In addition to considering representation at the state level, we considered representation by urban and rural classifications. Figure 3.7 depicts the percentage of public high schools in each census urban and rural classification that contain JROTC programs. Again, if the programs were equally represented in all classifications, we would expect these bars to be the same height. However, Figure 3.7 shows a distinct pattern in representativeness: Urban areas (particularly, large and mid-size cities) have higher-than-expected representation, and JROTC is less prevalent in areas that are classified as "rural, distant" and "rural, remote."[2] These are the rural areas that are farthest from urbanized areas and urban clusters. As noted, approximately 16 percent of public high schools in the United States have a JROTC unit. Only 7 percent and 2 percent of public high schools in "rural, distant" and "rural, remote" areas, respectively, have JROTC units. By contrast, 23 percent and 28 percent of public high schools in "city, large" and "city, mid-size" areas, respectively, have JROTC units.

Many of the same issues that may influence state-level representativeness play a role in the representativeness of JROTC programs in rural and urban areas. Rural areas contain smaller high schools, on average, compared with urban and suburban areas. Again, given lim-

---

[2] *Locale codes* describe a school's location in one of nine categories of location, ranging from "city, large" to "rural, remote." The codes are based on the physical location represented by an address that is matched against a geographic database maintained by the U.S. Census Bureau. Descriptions of each of the nine categories of locale codes may be found in NCES, "Identification of Rural Locales," undated.

Figure 3.3
Percentage of JROTC Units Sponsored by the Army Across U.S. States, 2015

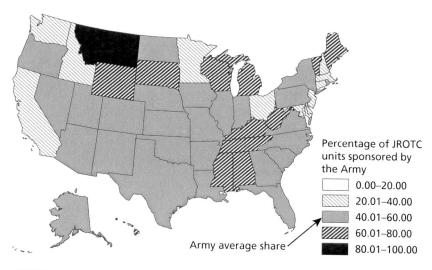

SOURCE: Project calculations from JROTC program data provided by the services in 2015 (NCES, undated-a).
RAND *RR1712-3.3*

Figure 3.4
Percentage of JROTC Units Sponsored by the Air Force Across U.S. States, 2015

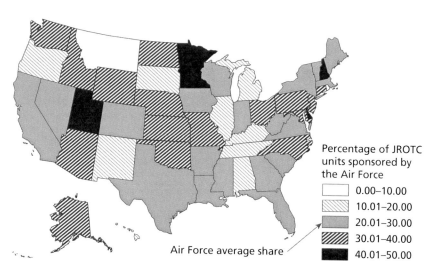

SOURCE: Project calculations from JROTC program data provided by the services in 2015 (NCES, undated-a).
RAND *RR1712-3.4*

Figure 3.5
Percentage of JROTC Units Sponsored by the Navy Across U.S. States, 2015

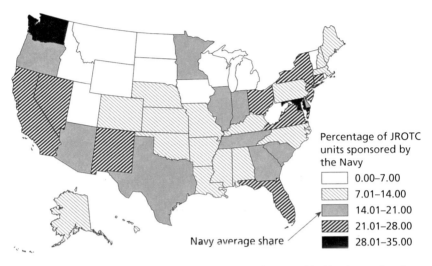

SOURCE: Project calculations from JROTC program data provided by the services in 2015 (NCES, undated-a).

RAND RR1712-3.5

Figure 3.6
Percentage of JROTC Units Sponsored by the Marine Corps Across U.S. States, 2015

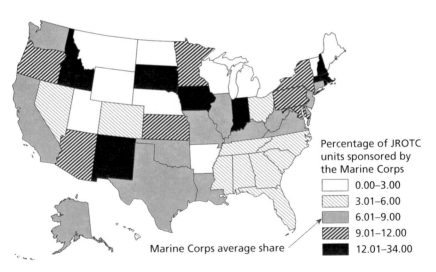

SOURCE: Project calculations from JROTC program data provided by the services in 2015 (NCES, undated-a).

RAND RR1712-3.6

Figure 3.7
Percentage of Public High Schools with JROTC Programs, by Urbanicity, 2015

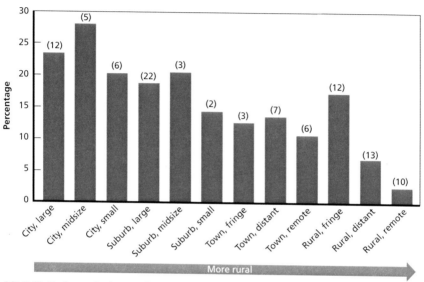

SOURCE: Project calculations from JROTC program data provided by the services in 2015.
NOTE: The number in parentheses indicates the percentage of all U.S. public high schools in the category.
RAND RR1712-3.7

ited resources and deep institutional knowledge about what makes programs successful and sustainable, achieving representativeness in rural areas may not be a priority for the services, and rural areas face several specific challenges to starting and sustaining JROTC programs. These challenges are discussed in detail in Chapter Four.

JROTC Programs Are Most Prevalent Among Medium and Large Schools and Underrepresented in Small Schools

Rural areas tend to have a much higher proportion of small schools, compared with urban and suburban areas. In fact, 69 percent of schools in rural areas have fewer than 500 students, compared with 44 percent in cities and 29 percent in suburbs. This is notable because JROTC programs are most prevalent in medium and large schools and under-represented in small schools (as defined in Figure 3.8). Twenty-six percent of schools with enrollment between 500 to 1,499 students have JROTC units, and 31 percent of schools with enrollment of at least 1,500 students have JROTC units. Fewer than 3 percent of schools with enrollment the smallest enrollment (fewer than 500 students) have JROTC programs.

JROTC Is Strongly Represented Among Schools Serving Economically Disadvantaged Populations

There is strong evidence that JROTC is well represented among schools serving economically disadvantaged populations, whether measured by

Figure 3.8
Percentage of High Schools with JROTC Programs, by Enrollment, 2015

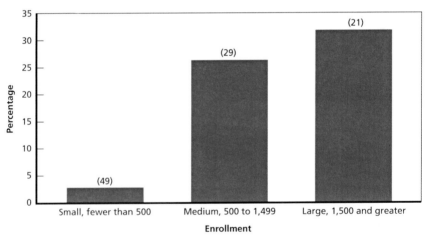

SOURCE: Project calculations from JROTC program data provided by the services in 2015 and the NCES Common Core of Data from the 2012–2013 school year (NCES, undated-a).
NOTE: The number in parentheses indicates the percentage of all U.S. public high schools in the category.
RAND RR1712-3.8

Figure 3.9
Percentage of Public High Schools with JROTC Programs, by Title I Eligibility, 2015

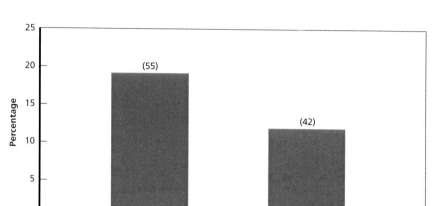

SOURCE: Project calculations from JROTC program data provided by the services in 2015 and the NCES Common Core of Data from the 2012–2013 school year (NCES, undated-a).
NOTE: The number in parentheses indicates the percentage of all U.S. public high schools in the category (3 percent of schools had missing data on Title I eligibility).
RAND RR1712-3.9

Title I eligibility or free and reduced-price lunch program participation. Figure 3.9 compares the percentage of Title I eligible public high schools that operate JROTC programs with those that are not eligible for Title I. Although 19 percent of Title I schools have JROTC units, only 12 percent of non–Title I schools have JROTC units. At public high schools with JROTC programs, 56.6 percent of students are eligible for free or reduced-price lunch, on average. At public high schools without JROTC programs, 46.9 percent of students are eligible for free or reduced-price lunch, on average. Taking both Title I eligibility and free and reduced-price lunch percentages into account, JROTC is well represented among high schools that serve economically disadvantaged communities. Because program objectives may weigh in favor of over-representation of disadvantaged students, this relative overrepresentation among schools serving economically disadvantaged populations is desirable. As detailed in Chapter Four, all four services consider Title I eligibility when selecting schools for JROTC-unit establishment.

JROTC Is Well Represented at Schools Serving Minority Populations

JROTC is well represented among public high schools with larger-than-average minority populations. Table 3.1 shows the school-average percentages of students in seven race and ethnicity categories. The first column shows these averages for schools operating JROTC programs, the second column shows these averages for schools not operating JROTC programs, and the final column shows the overall average for public high schools. In general, schools operating JROTC programs have higher-than-average representation for minority students and lower-than-average representation for white students. At public high schools with JROTC programs, 29.4 percent of students are African American. At non-JROTC schools, 12.1 percent of students are African American. At public high schools with JROTC programs, 22.4 percent of students are Hispanic. At non-JROTC public high schools, 19.7 percent of students are Hispanic. As with economic disadvantage, overrepresentation

Table 3.1
Percentage of Students in NCES Race/Ethnicity Categories for Public High Schools with JROTC, Public High Schools Without JROTC, and All Public High Schools, 2015

Race/Ethnicity	JROTC (%)	No JROTC (%)	All Public High Schools (%)
American Indian/Alaska Native	1.1	2.5	2.2
Asian	3.4	2.7	2.8
Hispanic of any race	22.4	19.7	20.1
African American	29.4	12.1	14.9
White	41.0	60.8	57.5
Hawaiian native/Pacific Islander	0.5	0.2	0.3
2 or more races	2.2	2.1	2.1

SOURCE: Project calculations from JROTC program data provided by the services in 2015 and the NCES Common Core of Data from the 2012–2013 school year.

NOTE: Totals might not sum to 100 because of rounding.

of schools serving minority populations may be desirable because of program objectives to prioritize schools serving disadvantaged populations. However, as we discuss in detail in Chapter Four, while all services consider Title I eligibility in selecting schools for JROTC unit establishment, only the Navy explicitly considers the minority share of the school population. The other three services do not include race and ethnicity measures in ranking schools, but their economic disadvantage measures are correlated with minority share.

Patterns in Representativeness May Reflect Prior Policy and Instructor Availability

Our findings are consistent with several past policy efforts by the services to increase the geographic and demographic representativeness of the JROTC program. In particular, Operation Young Citizen (Corbett and Coumbe, 2001) specified objectives to increase the demographic and geographic representativeness of the JROTC program; special efforts were made to open JROTC programs in schools that were economically disadvantaged or served at-risk youth and to expand the geographic reach of JROTC. Our findings on representativeness suggest that, although policy implemented to serve at-risk youth and increase demographic representativeness were successful, policy to increase geographic representativeness has not been successful.

With respect to instructor availability, service representatives suggested in our interviews that the concentration of military retirees within each state might affect JROTC unit distribution because states with larger retiree pools have more potential instructors. As detailed in Appendix B, we conducted regression analyses to examine whether there is a correlation between each state's percentage of the population who are veterans and the location of JROTC units, but we did not find a statistically significant relationship.[3] Service representatives also suggested that instructor availability might be related to proxim-

---

[3] Although data on military retirees would have been preferable for our analysis, only data on veterans were available.

ity to installations and facilities for veterans. We conducted a regression analysis to examine whether there is a relationship between the percentage of each state's area covered by military installations and the likelihood that high schools in that state host JROTC units, but we found no statistically significant relationship. More-nuanced analyses on instructor availability and installations—for example, a spatial analysis examining the relationship between the distance to the nearest military installation and JROTC unit distribution—may better explore this relationship. Unfortunately, we did not have access to such detailed data for this study.

At the School Level, Female Cadets Are Slightly Underrepresented

The demographic analyses in this chapter were at the school level, and our conclusions about representativeness reflect on whether the schools operating JROTC are representative of school-level demographics. However, an analysis of gender at the school level for high schools with JROTC units versus public high schools overall is not expected to yield useful results because there is little heterogeneity in gender composition across schools (i.e., schools are typically close to 50 percent male and 50 percent female).

Instead, we examine gender representativeness by comparing the average proportion of women participating in JROTC (across the services) to the average proportion of women across schools operating JROTC programs. According to 2016 service administrative data provided to us from the Army, the Air Force, the Marine Corps, and the Navy, approximately 40 percent of the cadets across each service's units are female. For comparison, in public high schools with JROTC programs, female students compose an average for 49 percent of students. This suggests that female students are slightly underrepresented in JROTC schools, compared with the student body as a whole. But considering that JROTC was previously limited to male enrollment (prior to 1972), today's share of female cadets does represent a significant achievement. It is also noteworthy that only 15 percent of the

DoD active-duty force is female (Office of the Deputy Assistant Secretary of Defense, 2014).

Summary

Compared with public high schools overall, JROTC is well represented among public high schools with larger-than-average minority populations. There is also evidence that JROTC is strongly represented in schools serving economically disadvantaged populations, whether measured by Title I eligibility or free and reduced-price lunch program participation. However, JROTC programs are far more prevalent in some states than in others, with a particular concentration in the Southeast. In addition, JROTC is underrepresented in rural areas.

CHAPTER FOUR

Factors That Affect the Initiation and Viability of JROTC Units

To identify opportunities for policy and practice to influence representativeness, we created a conceptual model to describe the factors that influence the creation and sustainment of JROTC units. We developed, by analyzing themes that arose through our literature review and interviews with school and service representatives, seven such factors:

- *School and community awareness*: To establish a unit, a high school must submit an application for a JROTC unit to one or more of the services. Thus, as a necessary condition to this process, a school or community must first become aware of JROTC and its benefits.
- *Community support*: Parents in communities that have positive opinions of JROTC or the military in general will be more likely to encourage their children to join JROTC. Through our interviews with principals and regional directors, we discovered that community support plays an important role in the success of cocurricular and extracurricular activities, and interview subjects noted that supportive communities typically provide more opportunities for extracurricular activities, such as parade participation.
- *School facilities*: According to principals and regional directors, school facilities are important because units must have space for activities, such as color guard, drill team, and marksmanship; storage facilities for uniforms, rifles, and other equipment; and classrooms to devote to JROTC instruction.

- *Instructor availability*: Services and school representatives and the literature on JROTC best practices reported that instructor quality is the most important factor in program success. Some schools have more difficulty recruiting and retaining talented instructors because the schools are in areas that are not as attractive to potential instructors.
- *Student participation*: Services require a minimum enrollment of either 10 percent of the number of students enrolled in the school who are in ninth grade or above or 100 students, whichever is less. Beyond minimum-enrollment requirements, the health of a unit relies on students taking on responsibilities, such as running drills and maintaining equipment. Successful units also rely on cadets who are eager to participate and take on leadership roles both in the classroom and in competitions and community service activities. Although JROTC regulations allow for a minimum enrollment of 100 students or 10 percent of the number of students enrolled in the school, school district and service representatives noted that units with fewer than 100 cadets would be inefficient because the unit would still be required to have two instructors. In addition, the school district and service representatives that we interviewed indicated that, without at least 100 cadets, smaller units would face difficulties in maintaining healthy units because cadets would be stretched too thinly across leadership roles, extracurricular activities, and competitions.
- *Funding*: Although the military services subsidize instructor salaries, uniforms, other equipment, curricular materials (including textbooks), and some travel costs, schools must contribute to instructors' salaries. In addition, schools must provide classroom and storage facilities for JROTC. If a school does not already have a classroom to devote to JROTC and storage facilities for uniforms and other equipment, the school will have to finance the construction of classroom and storage facilities for JROTC.
- *Selection and closures*: After a school applies to a service to request a JROTC unit, the service ranks the school candidate based on a number of defined factors, which vary by service. Once a school is selected for unit establishment, the sponsoring service and the

school district enter into the agreement that governs the administration of the unit. Services regularly review units for continuance or closure and may close units with low enrollment, that lack required resources, or that are out of compliance with other provisions of the agreement.

Service Policies and Initiatives Affect Three of the Factors

While our analysis found seven factors that are important in creating and sustaining JROTC units, we also found that services' policies and initiatives are most likely to affect three of the factors, as depicted in Figure 4.1: (1) school and community awareness, (2) instructor availability, and (3) selection and closures. Community support and student participation are less likely to be affected by service policy and initiatives because these factors are often tied to preexisting military sentiment within the community. School facilities are also a condition outside the services' control because they do not have funds to build classrooms, storage facilities, and drill areas for schools that wish to initiate the JROTC program. Service policies and initiative are also less

Figure 4.1
Three Factors Affected by Service Policies and Initiatives

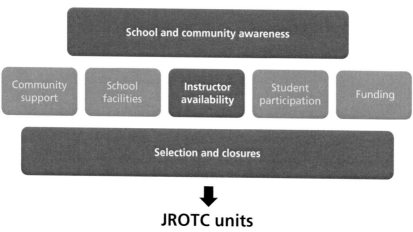

likely to affect funding outside financial support for instructor salaries because services and school districts must operate within their respective budget constraints. Therefore, the remainder of this section focuses on the three factors that services' policies and initiatives can most readily influence.

School and Community Awareness

Regional directors and principals reported that prospective schools most frequently learn about JROTC from existing programs in their areas. For example, during our interviews, high school principals reported that their desire to open JROTC units sprung from witnessing the leadership and community service opportunities that JROTC offered to neighboring schools. Schools in areas with high concentrations of JROTC units are, therefore, more likely to become aware of JROTC and its benefits. This network-effect type of phenomenon is likely partially responsible for the heavy geographic concentration of JROTC programs.

Some services conduct marketing and outreach to raise awareness in areas with no or few programs. The Air Force recently opened new units in Idaho and Montana after visiting schools in these states and networking with school districts. The Air Force's activity is a good example that any of the services could use to build awareness for JROTC if resources were available. Also, the Navy sent a letter to every school district in the United States when the Navy instituted its NDCC program in 2011 to raise awareness of the program among schools and school districts.

Instructor Availability

Services and school representatives reported in our interviews that instructor quality is the most important factor in program success. Literature on implementing JROTC and on best practices for JROTC units also focuses on instructor quality. Hanser and Robyn (2000) noted: "In several sites, retired military professionals charged with leading the program brought exceptional qualities of leadership, commitment, and perseverance to the job." Crawford, Thomas, and Estrada (2004) noted: "Like all good leaders, JROTC instructors at high-performing units are enthusiastic, tireless, and good role models. They set high standards and delegate meaningful work to the cadet chain of command."

While we found no quantitative evidence that instructor availability was related to the concentration of military retirees within each state or the proximity of installations and veterans' facilitates, service representative reported that some schools have more difficulty attracting and retaining talented instructors because the schools are located in areas that are not as attractive to military retirees. The service representatives reported that military retirees may be attracted to areas based on many factors, including

- quality of life
- salaries and cost of living
- commute time
- proximity to installations and veterans facilities.

If a school district is lacking in one or more of these factors, regional directors told us that it may be difficult to fill open JROTC instructor positions. This could lead to schools having to accept lower-quality instructors or enduring a lengthy period with a reduced number of instructors for the unit.

Services have similar policies on instructor qualifications. As noted, unless a temporary waiver has been obtained, senior instructors are retired active-duty officers and junior instructors are NCOs. All services allow retirement-eligible reservists and guard members to be certified as JROTC instructors. Each service certifies retired active-duty and reserve military personnel to be JROTC instructors, but instructors are hired by the school districts from the pool of certified instructors and are civilian employees of the school.

There are some differences among service policies on instructor qualifications and selection. The Army, the Air Force, and the Marine Corps only certify their own retirees as JROTC instructors. The Navy allows retirees from the Navy, the Marine Corps, and the Coast Guard to be certified as instructors for their JROTC units. All services except for the Navy provide recommendations of candidates that may be a good fit to school districts trying to fill instructor openings, although the school district is responsible for making the hiring decision.

Some services recently reduced instructor-salary support from 12 months to ten months. The Army adopted this policy for new hires only, and the Air Force adopted this policy for all instructors. Some regional directors reported reduced interest in rural areas and high-poverty urban areas because of these reduced instructor salaries. In addition, some service and school district representatives noted that, because JROTC instructors administer leadership camps and other trainings and extracurricular activities over the summer, a ten-month contract would not compensate instructors for the full year of work required to maintain a healthy unit.

Selection and Closures

After a school applies to a service for a JROTC unit, the service ranks the school candidate and places it on a school candidate list. The ranking is based on a number of defined factors, which vary by service. The Army, the Air Force, and the Navy use weighted point systems (with a total of 100 possible points), while the Marine Corps ranks schools based on factors without specific weighting. The candidate ranking factors are summarized in Table 4.1.

Notably, the relative weighting varies across services. The Air Force and Navy weight state representation most heavily (40 points). The Army assigns 15 points to state representation, and the Marine Corps uses state representations as one of its unweighted factors. For Title I eligibility, the Army allots 20 possible points, the Air Force and Navy allot five possible points, and the Marine Corps uses Title I eligibility as one of its unweighted factors. Whether a school is in a rural area is one unweighted factor that the Marine Corps considers, while schools in metropolitan areas receive up to five points under the Air Force's rubric.

According to 2016 service administrative data provided to RAND, there are 280 schools on the Army school candidate list, 243 schools on the Air Force list, 65 schools on the Marine Corps list, and 211 schools on the Navy list. Some schools may be on more than one service's school candidate list.

Table 4.1
School Candidate Ranking Factors for the Army, Air Force, Navy, and
Marine Corps, 2015

Category	Factor	Army	Air Force	Navy	Marine Corps
Geography	State representation	15	40	40	✓
	Rural area	—	—	—	✓
	Metropolitan area	—	5	—	—
	Instructor availability	—	15	—	—
School resources and support	School facilities	10	10	—	—
	Program support, credit hours for JROTC, type of schedule	15	15	10	✓
	Enrollment	15	(part of discretionary)	15	✓
	Financial solvency	5	—	—	—
	Time on waiting list	—	5	—	—
Representation	Title I eligibility	20	5	5	✓
	Indicators of need	20	(part of discretionary)	—	—
	College enrollment rate	—	—	10	—
	Share of racial/ ethnic minorities	—	—	20	—
	Discretionary	—	5	—	—
Total		100	100	100	N/A

SOURCE: Summary JROTC program data provided by the services in 2015.

NOTE: The Army, the Air Force, and the Navy use weighted point systems (with a total of 100 possible points), while the Marine Corps ranks schools based on factors without specific weighting.

After a school is selected for unit establishment, the sponsoring service and the school district enter into an agreement that governs the administration of the unit. As noted, agreements require, among other things, that the school maintain a minimum enrollment. Services regularly review units for continuance or closure, and units with low enrollment, that lack required resources, or that are out of compliance with other provisions of the agreement may be closed.

Seven Factors Play Unique Roles in Starting and Maintaining JROTC Programs in Rural Areas, Underrepresented States, and Economically Disadvantaged Schools

As detailed above, service policies may affect three factors involved with initiating and maintaining JROTC units—in particular, school and community awareness, instructor availability, and selection and closures. Our interviews with service and school district representatives helped to determine how these factors, as well as the other four factors (community support, school facilities, student participation, and funding), affect the establishment and maintenance of units in rural areas, underrepresented states (e.g., states with a smaller-than-average proportion of schools operating JROTC units), and economically disadvantaged schools. The sections that follow and Tables 4.2 to 4.4 explain the challenges and opportunities that schools face in relation to these seven factors.

Rural Areas

Table 4.2 summarizes the challenges and opportunities that school district representatives and regional directors reported that schools in rural areas face. According to these representatives, rural areas face challenges with respect to instructor availability because many instructors do not wish to relocate to rural areas. Representatives also noted that remote rural areas—isolated towns and small cities whose nearest population center is 50 to 100 miles away—face additional difficulties. School district and service representatives also noted that awareness is

Table 4.2
JROTC Challenges and Opportunities in Rural Areas

Factor		Challenge/Opportunity
Awareness	●	In remote rural areas, it is harder to learn about benefits of JROTC through nearby schools.
Community support	○	Units in rural areas report opportunities to participate in parades, and local newspapers give positive publicity.
School facilities	○	Quality of school facilities varies among rural units. Some remote, rural units may benefit from proximity to open spaces for drills.
Instructor availability	●	Rural areas are less attractive to military retirees.
Student participation	●	Extracurriculars and competitions draw students to JROTC. These activities are difficult to organize in remote rural areas because of distance to other units.
Funding		No specific challenge reported.
Selection and closures		In its selection criteria, the Air Force slightly disfavors rural schools, the Marine Corps favors rural schools, and the Army and the Navy do not consider rurality.

NOTE: Red circles indicate challenges, green circles indicate opportunities, and gray circles indicate neutral or no information about the factor.

an issue for schools in remote rural areas because geographic isolation prevents these schools from learning about JROTC and its benefits from neighboring schools. Student participation is also reportedly an issue for schools in remote, rural areas. Because units may be as far as 100 miles from the next-closest unit, competitions and extracurricular activities are difficult to organize. According to school district and service representatives, lack of organized competitions and events makes JROTC less attractive to students because competitions and extracurricular activities are a large part of the appeal of JROTC for many students.

Underrepresented States

Table 4.3 summarizes the challenges and opportunities that schools in underrepresented states face. According to school district and service representatives, generating awareness of JROTC is a challenge in states with a low concentration of JROTC units. As with schools in remote, rural areas, schools in underrepresented states are not as likely to learn about JROTC and its benefits from neighboring schools. Service and school district representatives also note that community support may be a challenge in underrepresented states where military sentiment is low. Low military sentiment and other quality-of-life factors may also make underrepresented states less attractive to military retirees, which in turn affects instructor availability. In addition, selection historically

Table 4.3
JROTC Challenges and Opportunities in Underrepresented States

Factor		Challenge/Opportunity
Awareness	●	In underrepresented states, it is harder for schools to learn about the benefits of JROTC from nearby schools.
Community support	●	In states where military sentiment is low, communities are less supportive of JROTC programs.
School facilities		No specific challenge reported.
Instructor availability	●	Some states are less attractive to military retirees.
Student participation		No specific challenge reported.
Funding		No specific challenge reported.
Selection and closures	●	Until recently, state representation was not considered in selection.

NOTE: Red circles indicate challenges, green circles indicate opportunities (not applicable for this table), and gray circles indicate neutral or no information about the factor.

posed a challenge for schools in underrepresented states because, until recently, state representation was not considered in selection.

Economically Disadvantaged Schools

Table 4.4 summarizes the challenges and opportunities that economically disadvantaged schools face. According to school district and service representatives, economically disadvantaged schools may face challenges with respect to school facilities because schools may not have drill areas available or classrooms to devote exclusively to JROTC. Representatives also reported that economically disadvantaged schools tend to be located in areas that are less attractive to military retirees,

Table 4.4
JROTC Challenges and Opportunities in Economically Disadvantaged Schools

Factor		Challenge or Opportunity
Awareness		No specific challenge reported.
Community support		No specific challenge reported.
School facilities	●	Economically disadvantaged schools might not have drill areas available or classrooms to devote exclusively to JROTC.
Instructor availability	●	Economically disadvantaged schools and high-poverty urban areas are less attractive to military retirees.
Student participation		No specific challenge reported.
Funding		No specific challenge reported.
Selection and closures	●	When scoring schools on the candidate list, all four services award points for Title I eligibility. The Army places the most weight on Title I.

NOTE: Red circles indicate challenges, green circles indicate opportunities, and gray circles indicate neutral or no information about the factor.

so instructor availability poses a challenge for these schools. However, as noted, when scoring schools on the school candidate lists, all four services award points for Title I eligibility, with the Army placing the most weight on Title I eligibility (see Table 4.1). Despite challenges posed by school facilities and instructor availability, JROTC is well represented among Title I schools.

Common Challenges for Rural Areas, Underrepresented States, and Economically Disadvantaged Schools

As noted in Chapter Three, our findings on demographic and geographic representativeness suggest that, although policies implemented to serve at-risk youth and increase demographic representativeness were successful, policies to increase geographic representativeness have not been successful. Rural areas and underrepresented states face common challenges: awareness, instructor availability, and student participation. In both of these geographically underrepresented areas, schools are unlikely to learn about benefits of JROTC through nearby schools because so few units exist. Instructor availability is also a common issue because these areas are unattractive to military retirees.

Schools in rural areas face an additional challenge with respect to student participation because aspects of JROTC that pique student interest, such as extracurriculars and competitions, are difficult to organize in remote, rural areas. Schools in underrepresented states face unique challenges because, in states where military sentiment is low, communities are less supportive of JROTC programs. In addition, until recently, state representation was not considered in selection, and therefore schools in underrepresented states were not prioritized in unit selection.

According to the service and school district representatives we interviewed, economically disadvantaged schools face difficulties recruiting instructors because the schools are often located in high-poverty urban areas, which are unattractive to military retirees.

As detailed in this chapter, of the seven factors that influence the creation and sustainment of JROTC units, services' policies and initiative are most likely to affect (1) school and community awareness, (2) instructor availability, and (3) selection and closures. In Chapter Five, we provide recommendations to increase geographic representativeness, which primarily focus on these three factors.

CHAPTER FIVE

Recommendations

This report had two purposes: examine geographic and demographic representativeness of JROTC programs and explore and describe how federal law, service policy, and school and community factors affect a school's capacity to start and successfully sustain JROTC units. In this chapter, we offer several policy recommendations to help promote representativeness.

It is important to consider the policy context under which our study was conducted. Specifically, this study was conducted when budget constraints faced by the individual services resulted in caps on the total number of JROTC programs that could be operated and maintained. All services currently operate at or near these caps, and, therefore, there is little room to increase representativeness by adding programs. This issue is compounded because there is little turnover in JROTC programs (see Table 5.1 for more details on planned units and trends in recent closures). Given the essentially stable number of programs, changes occur largely through closures and openings of units at a limited number of schools on the school candidate lists. Representativeness will be affected only gradually by these small changes in program distribution. This means that policy options to promote JROTC representation in underrepresented states and rural areas are limited. Nevertheless, we recommend eight potential actions that could help to promote representativeness, particularly in rural areas. These recommendations are presented below, along with some considerations for the potential positive and negative consequences of implementing these policy changes.

Table 5.1
Current JROTC Units, Planned JROTC Units, and Reasons for Recent
Closures, April 2016

	Army Units	Air Force Units	Navy Units	Marine Corps Units
Current units	1,701	878	573	236
Planned units	1,709	870–880	580	235
Reasons for recent closures	No units have been closed because of low enrollment; districts have closed some units because of funding	Ordinary review process (because of sustained low enrollment or program noncompliance)	Systematic effort to close about 60 units from 2011 to 2013 because of low enrollment	No units have been closed because of low enrollment; districts have closed some units because of funding

SOURCE: JROTC program data provided by the services in April 2016.

Use Program Alternatives, Such as NDCC, to Support Expansion in Rural Areas and Underrepresented States

NDCCs could be used to make room for new JROTC units within the existing unit caps. The services might be less hesitant to close under-enrolled JROTC units if these units could be transitioned to NDCC units. In other words, NDCC would be used as a soft landing for underenrolled JROTC units. Closure of these underenrolled units would make room for establishment of new JROTC units in under-represented states and rural areas. Each new closure would provide an opportunity for a school on the school candidate list located in an underrepresented state or rural area to open a unit.

NDCCs could also be promoted as an option for communities with the ability to fully fund units. It is uncertain whether schools in underrepresented areas would be able and willing to fully fund JROTC units, but some schools in traditionally overrepresented areas may be willing to fund NDCC units if it is the only way they can open new units. By expanding NDCC in whichever areas are able to fully fund units, the services will maintain their few openings in JROTC for underrepresented areas. If some of these new NDCC units are estab-lished in rural areas and underrepresented states, the services could prioritize them for transition to funded JROTC units when openings become available. However, for NDCC to be an effective tool for increasing JROTC units in underrepresented areas, JROTC transition criteria must reflect whether a unit is located in an underrepresented area. If criteria for transitioning schools from NDCC to JROTC do not favor schools in underrepresented states and rural areas, then services run the risk that openings will be filled by schools in geographically overrepresented areas.

In expanding the NDCC program, the services must be clear about whether and how NDCC affects chances of being awarded a JROTC unit in order to prevent buyer's remorse on the part of schools. Several service representatives noted that some schools decide to fund an NDCC in the short term in hopes that the school will quickly be transitioned to a JROTC unit. Schools that establish NDCC in hopes of transitioning to JROTC may resent long or indefinite waits, so upfront communication is crucial to align expectations about the possibility of transition to JROTC and any conditions required to become eligible for transition.

Raise Awareness of JROTC Programs to Increase Geographic Representativeness

The services have marketed JROTC to underrepresented areas by visiting schools in underrepresented states to network with school districts and by sending letters to school districts throughout the United States. As noted, the Air Force recently opened new units in Idaho and Montana after visiting schools in these states and networking with school districts. When it instituted its NDCC program in 2011, the Navy sent a letter to every school district in the United States to raise awareness.

If manpower and resources are available, the services could increase such marketing and outreach in rural areas and underrepresented states. These strategies might stimulate interest in areas with low military sentiment. Areas with low military sentiment and few JROTC units are likely less aware of the benefits of the program. Marketing efforts that emphasize the benefits of JROTC could stimulate interest in these areas. A marketing-strategy question for further exploration is what level of effort would be required to stimulate interest in regions with low JROTC density and low military sentiment. Sending letters emphasizing the benefits of JROTC would be a relatively low-effort, low-cost strategy. A higher-cost, higher-effort strategy would be to send regional directors to these areas to network with school district officials.

A separate marketing and outreach effort could be made with respect to potential JROTC instructors, a key component of successful JROTC units. These marketing and outreach efforts would be directed toward military retirees in underrepresented states and rural areas to increase instructor pools in these areas.

Consider Flexibility in Instructor Requirements for Rural Areas and Small Schools

When a senior-instructor position is hard to fill, the services will often allow an NCO to fill the position under a waiver. The services might consider a more routine process for hiring well-qualified NCOs with bachelor's degrees for senior-instructor positions. This approach could expand the pool of instructors for underrepresented states, rural areas, and low-income areas.

The services might also consider alternatives to the traditional model of two full-time JROTC instructors for small schools. The Navy and the Marine Corps allow for a 50-cadet minimum and one rather than two instructors for NDCC units. In addition, in small schools with lower JROTC enrollment, the services might consider agreeing to share JROTC instructors with other subject duties, if the JROTC program could be managed with two part-time instructors instead of two full-time ones. Department of Defense Instruction 1205.13 (2006) provides that high schools may "[c]ontract separately with the individual JROTC instructor for any additional duties desired by the institution besides instruction, operation, and administration of the JROTC Program, at no cost to the Military Department concerned. Such additional services shall be performed outside the scope of JROTC duties and hours." However, services may have to adopt policy changes to implement this more flexible approach. Currently, teaching non-JROTC math, social studies, or other subjects during the school's normal day of academic instruction appears to be prohibited by Army policy.[1] In addition, instructors would have to be credentialed by the school districts to teach additional subjects, and the services would have to work with schools to determine how much of a part-time JROTC instructor's salary would be reimbursed by the service.

Weigh the Benefits and Drawbacks of Changing Instructor-Salary Policy

As noted, some services recently reduced instructor-salary support to ten months instead of 12. A CNA report on Army JROTC instructor pay presents several alternatives that would reduce the amount of the JROTC budget devoted to instructor pay (Alper et al., 2015). These alternatives included ten-month contracts for all instructors, as well as several other options for restructuring instructor salaries. According to Alper et al. (2015), adoption of ten-month salaries by the Air Force and by the Army for new hires has not caused attrition. Services may find it attractive to reduce the cost of JROTC programs using these policies. However, service representatives noted in our interviews that adoption of ten-month instructor contracts may affect instructor interest in JROTC in general and may particularly affect interest in hard-to-fill locations. Service representatives also noted that, because instructors administer leadership camps over the summer and use summers to pre-

---

[1] The "frequently asked questions" section of the Army JROTC (AJROTC) employment portal states: "May the instructors teach non-AJROTC subjects, such as math or social studies? AJROTC instructors perform only those duties connected with the instruction, operation, and administration of the AJROTC program. Individuals employed as AJROTC instructors will not perform duties or teach classes in any discipline other than Army JROTC unless the performance of such duties or the teaching of such classes is outside the school's normal day of academic instruction and is contracted for between the school and the individual AJROTC instructor at no expense to the Army" (U.S. Army, undated).

pare curricula, compensating instructors for only ten months would not be practical.

One school district representative we spoke with noted that some districts compensate Air Force JROTC instructors for the full two months of salary not covered by the Air Force. However, it is not clear how widespread this practice is and how many school districts would be willing to pay an additional two full months of salary if the ten-month contract were adopted for all JROTC instructors.

Consider Changing and Standardizing Program Selection Criteria

The services and the Office of the Secretary of Defense may want to consider a more standardized approach to selection criteria (see Table 4.1), with similar weighting on key factors that affect demographic representativeness (e.g., Title I eligibility, indicators of need and share of racial and ethnic minorities) and geographic representation (e.g., state representation and rural versus metropolitan area). However, in formulating this approach, it is important to balance the goals of representativeness and program success. Some scoring criteria for school candidate lists may make it harder for schools in rural areas to rank highly, but these criteria are associated with program success. For example, school size is important for maintaining minimum-enrollment requirements, and instructor-management factors, such as quality of life and proximity to a metropolitan area, make possible the retention of good instructors. However, these factors may also weigh against rural schools and under-represented states. Thus, while changing selection criteria might benefit geographically underrepresented areas, these changes could raise risks to program sustainability.

Provide Remote Rural Schools with More Discretion in Allocating Travel Funding

Distribution of travel funds to units varies by service. The Navy and the Army distribute funds to units on a per-cadet basis. The Air Force distributes funds to units on a per-cadet basis and provides additional discretionary funds to regional directors. The Marine Corps distributes funds to regional directors on a regional per-cadet basis, and it is within the directors' discretion to distribute funds based on unit need (including NDCC units, which the other services do not fund).

If regional directors have the discretion to distribute travel funds, they could assist remote rural schools that are farther from competitions and extracurricular activities. However, any effects of this policy change would likely be marginal, because travel funds are limited.

Maintain Standardized Program Data That Can Be Easily Linked with External Data Sources

The data that we received from services were uniform; each data file included the address (with separate columns for street, city, state, and zip code), enrollment, and Title I status of all of the units sponsored by the service. In addition, all data appeared to be current. We recommend that the services continue to maintain consistent, timely, and comparable data. The services and the Office of the Secretary of Defense should agree on the exact data elements that each service should maintain and the appropriate definitions and formats.

As part of this process, we recommend that the services add NCES school identification numbers to JROTC program data to ease future analysis of demographic and geographic representativeness. As noted in Appendix B, all U.S. high schools are assigned a unique NCES number, and these identifiers are normally used to merge the Common Core of Data with other sources. The JROTC program data do not contain the NCES identification numbers. Adding NCES identification numbers to the services' program data would facilitate merging Common Core of Data with JROTC program data.

Consider Dedicated Funding for JROTC

As noted, Congress has expressed an interest in increasing the number of JROTC units. In fact, Congress articulated the desired expansion of JROTC in the National Defense Authorization Act for Fiscal Year 2009 (Public Law 110-417, 2008), which required the Secretary of Defense to develop a plan to establish and support 3,700 JROTC units by 2020. However, the services' budget constraints prevented unit expansion to this desired level. As of April 2016, the services were about 300 units short of the goal; there were 3,390 JROTC units at U.S. high schools.

If Congress desires expansion of JROTC, Congress should consider appropriating funds dedicated to JROTC. Currently, any additional funding appropriated to the services and any savings realized through JROTC service initiatives (such as adopting ten-month instructor contracts) do not have to be invested in JROTC. In other words, the services are under no obligation to use additional funds or savings to fund expansion of JROTC units. By appropriating dedicated funding for JROTC, Congress could ensure that sufficient funds are directed toward expanding JROTC in line with congressional intent. If such expansion is targeted to underrepresented states and rural areas, representation in such states and areas will increase.

CHAPTER SIX

Conclusion

JROTC serves more than 550,000 students each year, many of whom are at risk for failing academically or dropping out of school. JROTC programs are widely distributed. Programs operate in all 50 states, four U.S. territories, the District of Columbia, and Department of Defense Education Activity schools overseas. There has been recent congressional interest in whether the schools participating in JROTC programs are representative with respect to geographic area, with a special focus on whether rural areas are adequately represented as expressed in a Senate report (Senate Report 113-211, 2014).

In response to congressional interest, this report has two primary objectives. The first is to examine representativeness of JROTC at the school level with respect to geography and demographics. The second is to determine how federal laws and policies affect starting and sustaining JROTC units.

As detailed in Appendix B, we collected information on representativeness by merging JROTC program data with data on all public high schools in the United States from the NCES Common Core of Data. We interviewed service and school representatives to collect information on starting and sustaining JROTC units, as well as on the benefits of JROTC for the students, challenges with JROTC unit administration, and instructor hiring. We also reviewed literature on the academic and nonacademic benefits of JROTC participation.

In Chapter Two, we concluded that studies that examined academic outcomes found consistently positive associations between GPA and JROTC participation. JROTC participation was also associated with lower dropout rates and improved attendance. The evidence on other academic benefits, including graduation rates and improved performance on standardized tests (including statewide assessments), showed more-mixed results. Studies have also been conducted on non-academic benefits. One study (CSIS, 1999) examined discipline rates and found a positive association between improved student outcomes and JROTC participation. In addition, although our interviews noted that JROTC helps students develop good character, leadership skills, and positive relationships with adult role models, the literature on this topic has yielded mixed results—some studies found an association between JROTC participation and personal characteristics, and others found neutral or not statistically significant results. Other benefits of JROTC participation were mentioned frequently in interviews. According to high school principals and service representatives, JROTC provides a place for students who are not involved in athletics or the school band to be part of a student community and to participate in extracurricular activities. These interviewees also noted that JROTC provides volunteer opportunities that allow students to benefit the larger community outside school.

The results of our Chapter Three analysis of geographic and demographic representativeness suggest that JROTC has been more successful in addressing some kinds of representation than others. Compared with public high schools overall, JROTC is well represented among public high schools with larger-than-average minority populations. In general, schools operating JROTC programs have higher-than-average representation for minority students and lower-than-average representation for white students. There is also evidence that JROTC is strongly represented in schools serving economically disadvantaged populations, whether measured by Title I eligibility or free and reduced-price lunch program participation. Because we used school-level data for analyses, all inferences about representativeness are at the level of the school. If the services collected demographic information within each JROTC unit, these data could be compared with within-school data from the NCES Common Core of Data. This comparison would allow conclusions to be drawn about whether individual JROTC programs are representative of the student body at a particular school.

To identify opportunities for policy and practice to influence representativeness, we needed a model of the factors that influence the creation and sustainment of JROTC units. As detailed in Chapter Four, we identified seven factors that influence the creation and sustainment of JROTC units. Our literature review and interviews indicate that, in this multilayered process, services' policies and initiative are most likely to affect (1) school and community awareness, (2) instructor availability, and (3) selection and closures.

In Chapter Five, we provided eight recommendations focused on responding to the concerns raised, both directly and by extension, in the Senate report (Senate Report 113-211, 2014). Specifically, our recommendations focus on features of program selection and closure policies that affect the representation of rural areas and on factors that may be critical to sustaining successful programs in these areas. We focus our recommendations to increase geographic representativeness on the three factors most likely affected by service policies and initiative.

First, the services' use of program alternatives, such as NDCC, can influence selection and closure by making room for new JROTC units within the existing unit cap. Transitioning existing JROTC programs into NDCC or encouraging new programs in well-represented areas to adopt NDCC would make room for the establishment of new JROTC units in underrepresented states and rural areas. Second, instructor availability may be positively influenced through more flexibility in instructor requirements, alleviating staffing issues in some rural areas. Additionally, instructor availability might be negatively influenced by adoption of the ten-month instructor salary policy, as noted by some service representatives, and so changes to this policy could influence the ability of rural schools to staff programs. School and community awareness may be influenced through increased marketing efforts, and, since awareness of the program and its benefits is a critical step in establishing a program, raising awareness in underrepresented areas may serve as an important step in increasing program representation in these areas. Changing selection criteria across the services to give similar weighting to key factors that affect demographic and geographic representation could increase representation, but it could also entail trade-offs in the viability of programs. We also recommend that Congress consider appropriating funds dedicated to JROTC, which would help to ensure that sufficient funds are directed toward expanding JROTC in line with congressional intent. Finally, we recommend that the services maintain standardized program data that can be easily linked with external data sources. Standardizing data can increase the capacity of the services to evaluate the demographic and geographic representativeness of the programs and can enable the services to track representativeness over time and monitor changes in representation in rural areas. These approaches to data management could promote representativeness to some extent, even without specific policy changes.

Further examination of instructor availability is warranted. As noted in Chapter Five, service representatives suggested that the concentration of military retirees within each state might affect JROTC unit distribution because states with larger retiree pools would have more potential instructors. However, our initial regression analyses did not yield statistically significant relationships between veteran density and JROTC density within states or between military installations and a state's likelihood of hosting a JROTC unit. Further examination of the effect of instructor availability and military installation on geographic representativeness might prove fruitful, though. For example, an analysis examining the relationship between the distance to the nearest military installation and JROTC unit distribution might yield statistically significant results.

Literature Review

As we note in Appendix B, Stephanic (2010) prepared a literature review for DoD's Office of Accession Policy, which summarizes studies on the association between JROTC participation and student outcomes and JROTC participation and military enlistment. This appendix contains our updated and revised literature review.

This literature review identified 12 high-quality, rigorous studies,[1] all of which employed a comparison-group methodology to make inferences about the impacts of JROTC participation on academic and nonacademic outcomes. Furthermore, we found that ten of these 12 studies tried to control for selection bias instead of just using a general comparison approach. The number of schools included varied greatly between studies. Two of these studies included only one school, two studies included three schools, three studies included between four and seven schools, one study included 12 schools, and one study included 75 schools. Three studies used nationwide surveys of high school students.

The Effects of JROTC on Student Outcomes

Studies that attempted to determine the effects of JROTC on students were generally of two types: those that attempt to measure the impact on quantifiable outcomes in academic achievement (such as GPAs,

---

[1] The studies are William-Bonds, 2013; Biggs, 2010; Pema and Mehay, 2009a; Pema and Mehay, 2009b; Curran, 2007; Bulach, 2002; CSIS, 1999; Flowers, 1999; Bachmann, 1994; Roberts, 1991; Hawkins, 1988; and Seiverling, 1973.

scores on standardized tests, graduation rates, and attendance) and those that discuss more-qualitative effects (such as self-esteem, leadership, and citizenship). Of the studies reported here of both kinds, the vast majority find mostly positive effects of the JROTC program.

Pema and Mehay (2009b), attempting to link participation in JROTC to measurable outcomes, found that the JROTC program is associated with an increase in standardized test scores, especially for students who persist in the program. The study used data from the High School and Beyond survey (U.S. Department of Education, Institute of Education Sciences, and National Center for Education Statistics, 2001), which follows a representative sample of 14,825 sophomores from 1980 to 1992. The study found that program effects vary between short- and long-duration participants and between those who participate in the early grades versus those who participate in later grades. The authors found that participation in JROTC is associated with not only an improvement in test scores but also, for those who enroll early in the program, higher graduation rates. Those who join JROTC in the later grades displayed no changes in graduation rates. Pema and Mehay (2009b) stated that positive academic outcomes were most evident in cadets who were early and continuous participants in JROTC.

In an earlier study, using samples of 10,270 and 8,634 students from the High School and Beyond survey (U.S. Department of Education, Institute of Education Sciences, and National Center for Education Statistics, 2001) and the National Education Longitudinal Survey (U.S. Department of Education and National Center for Education Statistics, 1990), respectively, Pema and Mehay (2009a) found mixed results on the effects of the JROTC program on students' academic achievement. The authors explained this by stating, "[T]he limited academic effects of JROTC [found here and in other studies] are not unexpected since the program tends to me more vocational and extracurricular, rather than academic, in nature." They went on to state that the absence of program effects on academic outcomes also could be due to inadequate controls for the at-risk status of JROTC students. Yet Pema and Mehay did find that African American JROTC students (about one-third of all participants) had lower dropout rates (by 9 to 24 percentage points) and higher graduation rates (by 11 to 17 percentage points) than both white JROTC participants and African American nonparticipants. And female students in JROTC (about 40 percent of all participants) had higher self-esteem scores than both female non-participants and male enrollees.

Using the Pema and Mehay (2009a) data set, Curran (2007) also examined the effect of JROTC on student achievement. He, too, emphasized the fact that a relatively large proportion of the JROTC enrollment is composed of at-risk youth. Statistically controlling for this, he concluded that JROTC does have a positive effect on high school youth—the primary goal of the program. In terms of GPA, absenteeism, standardized test scores, and high school graduation, Curran found that JROTC students performed better than they would have been expected to perform without the program; that is, JROTC brought them up to where their performance equaled that of the non-JROTC participants.

CSIS (1999) examined similar student outcomes in its study of three school systems supporting the Army JROTC. The schools were chosen according to various criteria: Chicago because of its size and diversity; Washington, D.C., because of its at-risk student popula-tion; and El Paso, Texas, because of its high proportion of Hispanic students. Using student surveys and focus groups, the authors found mostly positive student outcomes in measurable metrics.

For the Army JROTC schools studied in Chicago, JROTC stu-dents had a lower dropout rate in 30 of 33 schools; a lower or equal suspension rate in 29 of 31 schools; a higher or equal graduation rate in 27 of 33 schools; a higher or equal GPA in 32 of 33 schools; and, for seniors, higher or equal ACT scores in all schools. Further, a survey of principals of these high schools found that they were knowledgeable about JROTC. Between 79 and 100 percent of principals rated the fol-lowing JROTC qualities as "excellent": improving self-esteem, value to school, value to students, instructors' abilities, presentation techniques and learning environment, and content of curriculum.

In terms of the Washington, D.C., school system, JROTC stu-dents had higher GPAs (2.3 average) than non-JROTC students did (2.2 average), higher SAT scores (754 versus 745), and a higher daily attendance rate (83 percent versus 63 percent). For the El Paso schools, JROTC students had higher average attendance rates and fewer infractions, although lower GPAs than non-JROTC students.

Biggs (2010) used data on 146 students (73 JROTC students and 73 non-JROTC students) at four Missouri high schools to compare JROTC students and non-JROTC students on measurements of student achievement, high school graduation, college enrollment, and enlistment rates. The study found no significant differences in academic achievement, high school graduation, or college enrollment.

William-Bonds (2013) compared JROTC students, non-JROTC student athletes, and other non-JROTC students at one urban high school in the Midwest to determine whether there were any differences in academic achievement. The study identified participants with similar GPAs from the school's 11th-grade population and randomly selected from this group 30 students from each of the three groups of interest. The study compared the students' standardized tests scores and self-perceptions of leadership and citizenship traits through a Likert-scale survey. The study found no significant difference in academic achievement using standardized assessments measured between 11th-grade JROTC students, student athletes, and other students. The study also found no significant difference in the students' perceptions of their leadership skills.

Perception of the impact of the mission and vision of JROTC has generated growing interest in the program. In a study conducted in Pennsylvania's public secondary schools in the early 1970s, Seiverling (1973) investigated the effectiveness of JROTC in relationship to three desired outcomes: leadership, citizenship, and self-reliance. He used the Gordon Personal Profile to measure leadership; the Pennsylvania Student Questionnaire (Secondary), Section F, to measure citizenship; and the Self-Concept as a Learner Scale to measure self-reliance. Seiverling compared 97 JROTC seniors with 97 non-JROTC seniors at a total of 12 public high schools and found no significant difference between the mean scores of JROTC cadets verses non-JROTC seniors on any of the three outcomes. It must be noted that this study was conducted almost 45 years ago, when the JROTC program was very different in structure and scope.

More significantly, in a later study, Hawkins (1988) measured the same outcomes as the earlier Seiverling study. Hawkins compared 83 senior Army JROTC cadets, who had been enrolled in JROTC for at least two years, with 92 seniors who were not taught JROTC courses in seven public secondary schools located in central Virginia. He found that JROTC cadets scored higher than non-JROTC cadets did on all three variables. Like Seiverling, Hawkins used the same measure of citizenship but used Stogdill's Leader Behavior Questionnaire (Form XII) (1963) to measure leadership and used the California Test of Personality (Thorpe, 1953) to measure self-reliance.

In a study conducted in Nevada, Roberts (1991) compared 59 Army JROTC seniors with 59 non-JROTC students at six high schools. In contrast to the cadets in earlier studies, the cadets in Roberts's study had been enrolled in JROTC for a minimum of four years. In this study, JROTC students scored significantly higher than their non-JROTC counterparts did on measures of citizenship, leadership, and self-reliance.

Bachmann (1994) found that JROTC participation may significantly increase self-esteem scores for some students. Bachmann analyzed the effects of participation in an Army JROTC program on leadership behavior and self-esteem for 94 high school juniors in three high schools in California, who had been enrolled in JROTC for at least two years, compared with 47 students from a comparable, yet non-JROTC, demographic. Results indicated that JROTC students scored significantly higher on measures of leadership and self-esteem. Male JROTC students scored significantly higher than non-JROTC males did in leadership, yet no significant difference was found in their scores for self-esteem. However, female JROTC students scored significantly higher than their non-JROTC counterparts did on measures of self-esteem, but no significant difference was found in their scores for leadership.

Similarly, Rivas (1995) measured self-esteem and learning skills in JROTC students. The target population was 117 male and female students attending four high schools in Illinois and Michigan. Rivas surveyed only first-year JROTC cadets at the two high schools in Michigan and surveyed only third- and fourth-year JROTC cadets at the schools in Illinois. Results showed that students in the first-year JROTC program scored significantly lower than the students did in their third and fourth years of JROTC on measures of self-esteem and learning skills. At a six-month posttest survey, results indicated that measures of self-esteem increased for all students, but only the first-year cadets showed gains on learning skills. In contrast to Bachmann (1994), Rivas found no gender bias in his results, suggesting that everyone may benefit equally from JROTC.

An interesting study of the perceptions about the claims of benefits to students enrolled in JROTC was conducted by Perusse (1997). Specific to JROTC units in Virginia and utilizing survey and interview data, Perusse investigated the perceptions of school counselors. This focus was based on the pivotal role that school counselors play in helping students select courses and plan an appropriate sequence of study. Given that the JROTC program at each school must maintain a required level of enrollment to remain a viable unit, and that JROTC instructors rely on support from their school administrators and school counselors, Perusse's study appears to have relevance, in that her findings indicated that school counselors were knowledgeable about the relationship between JROTC and the military, were in general agreement with the claims of benefits to students, and indicated a positive attitude about these benefits to students. Counselors identified specific characteristics of students for whom they would recommend JROTC as an appropriate elective, as well as for whom it may not be appropriate or feasible. Perusse concluded that school counselors in Virginia had a generally positive perception toward JROTC in Virginia public schools.

An additional perception survey conducted in North Carolina high schools by Morris (2003) asked principals to respond to 24 statements using a Likert scale; seven demographic questions about the JROTC program; and ten questions about the principal's school and perceptions about JROTC. A total of 344 surveys were mailed to the principals of North Carolina high schools, and 184 were returned, representing a 53-percent response rate. The demographic information indicated that 50 percent of the JROTC units were sponsored by the Army, the JROTC programs primarily attracted students with GPAs between 2.1 and 3.5, and most of the JROTC instructors were male and had received a standard or outstanding rating on teaching performance. The perception data went on to indicate that the principals agreed that cadets benefited from the JROTC programs, especially in the areas of leadership, citizenship, and teamwork.

A 1999 study surveyed 57 Army JROTC sophomores and 57 non-JROTC sophomores at three high schools to compare their leadership behavior, self-esteem, attendance, and out-of-school suspensions (Flowers, 1999). Flowers surveyed the students using a standardized questionnaire to determine leadership behavior, a second questionnaire to determine a measure of self-esteem, and a third to determine demographic information. Flowers also collected attendance and out-of-school suspension data from the school administrations. Analysis indicated a statistically significant difference between JROTC and non-JROTC sophomores for leadership scores and daily attendance, with JROTC students scoring higher on both measures. Data analysis also indicated that there was not a statistical difference between out-of-school suspensions between the two groups. Flowers questioned the results of the measure of self-esteem, because his results were not consistent with other studies that indicated higher self-esteem scores, particularly among females.

Schmidt (2001) administered the Personal Development Test (PDT) (Cassel, 2001) to 64 Marine JROTC cadets. The PDT measured personal maturity and social integration. His findings compared the results of the cadet responses with typical high school students; he found that the cadets tested higher in each of 13 PDT scores and statistically higher in eight PDT scores. Female and male cadets were only statistically different in the sympathy score (female cadets showed more sympathy than male cadets did).

In a later study, Schmidt (2003) reported that JROTC performance on the PDT suggested that carefully organized team membership, as in participation in JROTC, tended to foster personal development in the individuals involved. Schmidt further suggested that high school dropouts were more likely to become incarcerated and that students in prisons were seriously lacking in personal development, thus suggesting that JROTC is a viable "delinquency prevention" program.

On the PDT, Schmidt compared 122 JROTC high school cadets from California with typical high school students from the United States and Canada. Results showed that a single score (sympathy) was the only significant difference between male and female students, favoring women and supporting Schmidt's earlier findings. Schmidt also found that students' scores were statistically significant, favoring JROTC cadets, in all categories of the PDT except team member and self-esteem.

Bulach (2002) surveyed a group of 277 JROTC students and 200 non-JROTC students in grades nine through 12 at a high school in Atlanta, Georgia, to explore differences in certain character traits, such as self-respect, honesty, discipline, and integrity. Bulach found that scores for JROTC students were superior for 94 out of 96 behaviors studied.

A sampling of 59 Air Force JROTC students was conducted by Karuiki and Williams (2006) at Sullivan South High School near Kingsport, Tennessee. The authors intended to determine whether there was a relationship between character traits (as found in character education programs, such as JROTC) and academic performance, as measured by GPA. This study utilized a modification of the What Do You Really Believe survey, developed by Phi Delta Kappa (Grubb, 1998). The modification changed Likert-scaled responses to yes or no responses and surveyed the following categories: honesty, responsibility, moral behavior, and ethics. The results of this study indicated a significant correlation in the relationship between character traits and academic performance. The authors concluded:

> The JROTC programs emphasize discipline, responsibility, and doing the right thing. For students to achieve in high school, they need discipline to complete homework on time and study for tests. High school students need to take responsibility for their learning by prioritizing their activities. Students with high character traits have the discipline to study, participate in meaningful extracurricular activities, and take responsibility for their success. The JROTC programs in schools continually emphasize discipline and responsibility, and provide a structured program which encourages students to strengthen these traits.

In addition, Kariuki and Williams found that honesty, responsibility, moral behavior, and ethics had a significant impact on the character traits of JROTC students.

JROTC and Military Enlistment

Despite the fact that JROTC is not a recruitment program, some studies included a discussion of the relationship between JROTC and military enlistments. Pema and Mehay (2009b) found positive enlistment effects for students who participated in early grades and persisted in the program. The authors further indicated that, although overall enlistment rates of the graduating class were higher in schools hosting JROTC than in schools that did not, less than a third of the students with some participation in JROTC actually enlisted, and only about 10 percent of the graduating class in JROTC schools enlisted in the military. By design, the program allows students to join JROTC at any point in high school. Those who completed at least three years of JROTC and who chose to enlist received a higher pay grade upon entry into the military.

Pema and Mehay (2009a) reported that JROTC has a sorting effect that channels students into the military and away from postsecondary education, because enlisting in the military and pursuing postsecondary education are mutually exclusive decisions. Pema and Mehay went on to explain that this result applied only to the average JROTC student enrolled in a typical JROTC school. They also indicated that most students who enrolled in JROTC did not complete the four-year program.

Pema and Mehay (2009c) examined the career effects of occupation-related vocational education, contributing to the research measuring the impact of secondary vocational education on labor market outcomes. The authors reported that prior studies revealed mixed results on the impact of vocational education on graduates' labor market success, which have divergent policy implications, and highlighted the need to better understand the pathways in which secondary vocational education affects labor market outcomes. The Pema and Mehay study used longitudinal data that attempted to capture the careers of military recruits who completed high school military science classes in the JROTC program, which align similarly to both vocational training and school-to-career programs. Pema and Mehay reported that, although JROTC shares elements of both vocational education and school-to-work programs, JROTC has often been overlooked or excluded by researchers. Pema and Mehay reported that the U.S. Department of Education classifies high school military science classes as "enrichment/other" rather than vocational education. Pema and Mehay contested this designation because it appears to contradict the Department of Education's definition of career technical education as classes that teach skills required in specific occupations and career clusters. The authors went on to describe the scope and content of JROTC, the use of military instructors, and the close link with the employer (the U.S. military) as evidence of the program's occupational orientation.

Nonetheless, the Pema and Mehay (2009c) study analyzed the impact of vocational education for employees in a single, broad occupational category. The analysis exploited the specific JROTC high school military science program and the unique link between JROTC and the military as a potential employer. Pema and Mehay used a military data set of new recruits who entered the military and compared the turnover and job performance of new hires with and without JROTC backgrounds. The researchers utilized pooled data on all recruit cohorts who entered the Navy between 1994 and 2001 under four-year contracts and with no prior military service. All JROTC recruits in the data set had earned at least three credits in high school military science.

Using this data set, Pema and Mehay (2009c) analyzed measures of career progression and job-match quality. Job-match quality was investigated based on (1) early turnover behavior during a recruit's four-year contract term and (2) voluntary reenlistment decisions at the expiration of the four-year contract. Career progression utilized objective measures of productivity based on promotion during the four-year contract. Pema and Mehay reported that most recruits enter in grades E-1 through E-3, where advancement is awarded administratively. Advanced grades are awarded for a number of reasons, including completion of JROTC. The researchers indicated that promotion to

E-4 represents expected career advancement during the first enlistment term, whereas promotion to E-5 reflects exceptional job performance and progression.

Analysis of the data set indicate that promotion rates for vocational trainees (those completing at least three credits of JROTC Naval Science) are similar to those of their peers, suggesting that vocational education does not directly increase job performance. However, Pema and Mehay (2009c) found that the occupational-specific training received through JROTC may reduce early turnover and improve long-range job stability for those who join the military, suggesting that one effect of participation in JROTC and enlistment is increased job-match quality.

As noted, Biggs (2010) used data on 146 students (73 JROTC students and 73 non-JROTC students) at four Missouri high schools to compare JROTC students and non-JROTC students on measurements of student achievement, high school graduation, college enrollment, and enlistment rates. The study found a statistically significant difference in the higher rate of enlistment among JROTC students.

Days and Ang (2004) employed a number of econometric models on High School and Beyond survey data from 1980 for the sophomore and senior cohorts. There were 74,125 observations for the sophomore cohort and 47,980 observations for the 1980 senior cohort. Day and Ang found that, although results showed that JROTC positively influenced enlistment when JROTC participation was treated as exogenous for both high school seniors and sophomores, the impact of JROTC participation on military enlistment decisions became negligible when self-selection into the JROTC program of high school students was taken into account.

Study Methods

In this appendix, we provide details on the study methods. The appendix begins with a discussion of the quantitative methods we used to analyze geographic and demographic representativeness, including our data sources and analysis approach. We then present details on the qualitative methods we used to investigate the benefits of JROTC, as well as facilitators and barriers to successful program operation. Finally, we discuss how we reviewed the literature on JROTC programs.

Geographic and Demographic Representativeness

Sample and Data Sources
To examine the geographic and demographic representativeness of JROTC, we needed data on (1) the location, demographics, high school affiliation, and service affiliation of each JROTC unit and (2) the location, demographics, and enrollment of all public high schools in the United States. JROTC program data were provided to us by the services and included location data for both JROTC and NDCC units. We used the Common Core of Data collected and housed by the NCES, part of the U.S. Department of Education, as the source of information on U.S. high schools. This data source includes both school-level geographic and demographic information about every public high school in the United States. For our analysis, we used the latest complete Common Core of Data file, from the 2012–2013 school year. A limitation of this data source is that it does not include private high schools. There are data sources that contain demographic information

on private high schools, but they include only samples of the private high school population. Thus, these potential sources are not useful in providing a full universe of potential JROTC locations. A mitigating factor to this limitation is that the vast majority of JROTC units are located in public high schools, with only a handful of units located in private (often military-themed) high schools.

All U.S. high schools are assigned a unique NCES identification number, and these identifiers are commonly used to merge the Common Core of Data with other sources. The JROTC program data do not contain the NCES identifiers, so we had to devise an alternate procedure. We used zip codes as a first step to match JROTC programs to entries in the Common Core of Data. In many cases, there is only one public high school in a given zip code, so this match is straightforward. But in some cases, there were multiple schools within a zip code. We hand-checked and matched all records with these types of ambiguities, using additional information, such as school names, to resolve the ambiguities. To ease future analysis, we recommend that the services add NCES identifiers to their program data. Our final data set contained records for 21,227 public high schools (both JROTC and non-JROTC).

Because this study used school-level data for analyses, all inferences about representativeness are at the level of the school: We can draw no conclusions about within-school representativeness and whether the students enrolled in a specific JROTC unit are representative of the student body at that school.

Analysis
Once the data set was constructed, we calculated summary statistics for JROTC and non-JROTC high schools. These included demographic statistics (racial and ethnic composition of the school, percentage of students on free or reduced-price lunch [a measure of poverty], and enrollment size) and geographic statistics (state, census region, and urbanicity of the school location). To measure representativeness, we compared the percentage of schools with and without JROTC units across different demographic and geographic categories. We also used these data to construct color-shaded (choropleth) maps using GIS soft-

ware. The variation in color-shading on these maps allowed us to analyze geographic representativeness, with more variation indicating less representativeness.

We also analyzed (1) the relationship between military presence within each state and JROTC unit distribution and (2) veteran population within each state and JROTC unit distribution. (Although data on military retirees would have been preferable for our analysis, only data on veterans were available.) Service representatives suggested that military presence in a state might be positively correlated with JROTC density within the state. Service representatives also suggested that the concentration of military retirees within each state might affect JROTC unit distribution because states with larger retiree pools would have more potential instructors.

To examine the relationship between military presence and the location of JROTC units, we used a database of DoD sites, as reported in the DoD 2010 Base Structure Report (which includes installations, ranges, and training areas) to calculate the percentage of each state's area covered by military installations (Office of the Deputy Under Secretary of Defense, 2010). This percentage served as the independent variable in a logistic regression predicting the presence of a JROTC unit at a particular school.[1] To account for the clustering of schools within states, we clustered our standard errors at the state level. We did not find a statistically significant relationship at the 0.05 level.

We also performed simple ordinary least squares regressions examining the relationship between

1. the percentage of public high schools with JROTC programs in each state and the percentage of the state's area that is made up of military bases
2. the percentage of JROTC programs in each state that is sponsored by the Air Force and the percentage of the state's area that is made up of Air Force military bases

---

[1] Logistic regression is appropriate for binary outcome variables. In the current analysis, our outcome was a binary variable indicating the presence ($y = 1$) or absence ($y = 0$) of a JROTC unit at a school.

3. the percentage of JROTC programs in each state that is sponsored by the Army and the percentage of the state's area that is made up of Army military bases

4. the percentage of JROTC programs in each state that is sponsored by the Marine Corps and the percentage of the state's area that is made up of Marine Corps military bases

5. the percentage of JROTC programs in each state that is sponsored by the Navy and the percentage of the state's area that is made up of Navy military bases.

Only the relationship between the percentage of public high schools with JROTC programs in each state and the percentage of the state's area that is made up of military bases was statistically significant at the 0.05 level.

To examine the relationship between veteran population and the location of JROTC units, we used data on the percentage of the civilian population 18 years and older who are veterans in each state (reported in the 2014 American Community Survey; see U.S. Census Bureau, 2014). This percentage served as the independent variable in a logistic regression predicting the presence of a JROTC unit at a particular school. To account for the clustering of schools within states, we clustered our standard errors at the state level. We did not find a statistically significant relationship at the 0.05 level. We also performed a simple ordinary least squares regression examining the relationship between the percentage of public high schools in each state that have JROTC programs and the percentage of the civilian population 18 years and older who are veterans in each state. We did not find a statistically significant relationship at the 0.05 level.

No additional variables were included in these four regressions, so the coefficients we obtained represent unstandardized correlation coefficients.

Benefits of JROTC and Barriers to and Facilitators of Program Operation

We used qualitative methods to investigate the benefits of JROTC, as well as the barriers to and facilitators of successful program operation. JROTC operates in specific, local contexts, and the programs are enacted by unique sets of actors. Additionally, program operation involves a wide range of stakeholders—from both the civilian and military sectors—including instructors, principals, and JROTC regional directors. We visited a small set of schools operating JROTC programs and complemented these site visits with semistructured interviews with key stakeholders. More information about how sites were selected for visits, as well as the interview process, is provided below.

Sampling

Because the study timeline did not allow us to request Paperwork Reduction Act (PRA) clearance, federal law limited us to including no more than nine non-DoD staff in interviews. To include the greatest number of schools within this limitation, we decided to interview one representative per school or district in a total of eight schools and one large district.

We purposively sampled schools (and the one district) to participate in this study using a two-tiered approach, aiming to include a variety of urban, suburban, and rural settings across different states and services and including both JROTC and NDCC programs. First, the services provided recommendations for schools to visit. Second, we selected additional sites for visitation that operated JROTC programs and were located in rural areas. This resulted in the selection of three sites that we visited. These included one densely populated suburban area and two different rural areas.

In addition, we conducted telephone interviews with principals and school district officials from JROTC and NDCC sites we did not visit (six in total). The one district we interviewed was recommended by the services because it has many JROTC programs and has a dedicated district staff person who coordinates all JROTC activity in the district, so we had the opportunity to gain a valuable cross-school perspective.

All interview subjects were drawn from a wide variety of geographic areas and were allocated across the four services as evenly as possible.

PRA restrictions do not apply to DoD employees, so we were able to interview more people in these groups. Specifically, we worked closely with the four service JROTC headquarters, conducting at least two group telephone discussions with each service. We also interviewed 14 regional directors. The regional director role varies by service but in all cases manages the JROTC unit administration for all units in an assigned geographic area. Finally, we interviewed representatives from the service headquarters for each of the four services. These individuals are responsible for the management of all JROTC units for their respective services and devise and implement service-wide JROTC policy.

Data Collection
Site Visits
We visited three schools with JROTC programs. One school was selected by regional directors, and the other schools were selected by the research team to represent rural areas. This was particularly important given our focus on geographic representativeness and the potential obstacles to initiating and maintaining successful JROTC programs in rural areas. The objective of these site visits was to document individual experiences with administering JROTC programs, as well as the specific challenges (and opportunities) that the rural context posed to successful program operation. A team of four RAND researchers spent one day at each school. During each visit, we met individually with the school principal, observed multiple JROTC classes and extracurricular activities, and toured the facilities.

Interviews
We developed semistructured interview protocols to gather information about the perceived benefits of JROTC, as well as the barriers and facilitators of successful program operation. Semistructured protocols allow for cross-case comparisons and for deeper exploration of specific issues. Each category of stakeholder (principal, district representative, regional director) had a specific interview protocol that was tailored

to accommodate different perspectives on program operations: Principals were asked more-detailed questions about program operations on a day-to-day basis, and regional directors were asked more questions about the larger landscape of programs in a particular region.

The interviews covered several topics, including the benefits of JROTC for students and for schools, challenges of JROTC unit administration, JROTC instructor hiring, and awareness of and feasibility of NDCC. We asked regional directors and service JROTC headquarters representatives about some additional topics, including urban and rural distribution of units, unique challenges for rural units, policies for struggling units and unit closure, and financial support.

Analysis

We analyzed our interview notes and the notes from our site visits to examine the benefits of JROTC participation and to develop a conceptual model of the factors that are important in creating and sustaining JROTC units.

To do this, we generally followed the approach of Eisenhardt (1989). We began by analyzing the within-case data to become familiar with each school, district, and region, and we then documented and described the unique challenges and practices encountered by each stakeholder. We then looked for common themes by investigating similarities and differences that arose across cases. These themes were used to shape our conceptual model. Finally, we compared and contrasted our conceptual model with existing literature (see the literature review below) to revise our model where necessary.

Literature Review

In 2010, Stephanic prepared a literature review for the DoD Office of Accession Policy (Stephanic, 2010), which summarizes studies on the association between JROTC and student outcomes and between JROTC and military enlistment. Additional studies were added to that review by Alper et al. (2015). We updated and revised Stephanic (2010), following several steps. Because we wanted to summarize evidence of JROTC's benefits compared with other high school experiences, we eliminated studies that examined only JROTC participants. The remaining studies all included some type of comparison group. We also reviewed copies of the actual studies cited by Stephanic,[2] and we made revisions to the descriptions of the studies where relevant. In addition to these revisions, we updated Stephanic's list to include studies that were conducted after 2010. We conducted a search of post-2010 studies on the association between JROTC and student outcomes and military enlistment. We used Google Scholar to locate studies published between 2010 and 2016 with the terms *JROTC, Junior ROTC, Junior Reserve Officers' Training Corps, Junior Reserve Officers Training Corps*, or *Junior Reserve Officer Training Corps* in the title. We found 23 studies. Among these 23 studies, we found 13 studies that examined the association between JROTC participation or student outcomes and JROTC participation and military enlistment. We then excluded ten studies that did not include a comparison group or did not control for selection bias. Three studies remained—one on student outcomes (William-Bonds, 2013), one on military enlistment (Days and Ang, 2004), and one on both student outcomes and military enlistment (Biggs, 2010). We added these three studies to the studies cited in Stephanic (2010).[3] We also reviewed Alper et al. (2015) and added two studies referenced there to the revised and updated literature review (Elliot, Hanser, and Gilroy, 2002; and Days and Ang, 2004). In total, the revised and updated literature review identified 12 high-quality, rigorous studies, all of which employed a comparison-group methodology to make inferences about the impacts of JROTC programs.[4] Appendix A contains the updated and revised literature review.

---

[2] Two studies, Curran (2007) and Bachmann (1994), were not available to us. We relied on Stephanic's summaries of these studies.

[3] The studies on student outcomes were Pema and Mehay, 2009a; Pema and Mehay, 2009b; Curran, 2007; CSIS, 1999; Seiverling, 1973; Hawkins, 1988; Roberts, 1991; Bachmann, 1994; Flowers, 1999; and Bulach, 2002. The studies on enlistment were Pema and Mehay, 2009a, and Pema and Mehay, 2009b.

[4] The studies are William-Bonds, 2013; Biggs, 2010; Pema and Mehay, 2009a; Pema and Mehay, 2009b; Curran, 2007; Bulach, 2002; CSIS, 1999; Flowers, 1999; Bachmann, 1994; Roberts, 1991; Hawkins, 1988; and Seiverling, 1973.

Limitations

Our quantitative and qualitative analyses were subject to certain limitations. This study uses school-level data for analyses, and all inferences about representativeness are at the level of the school. We can draw no conclusions about within-school representativeness and whether the students enrolled in a specific JROTC unit are representative of the student body at that school.

The Common Core of Data does not include private high schools. Although there are data sources that contain demographic information on private high schools, they include only samples of the private high school population and were therefore not suitable for our analysis.

As detailed above, we conducted regression analyses using data on location of JROTC units, the percentage of the population who are veterans in each state, and the percentage of each state's area covered by military installations. With the exception of the ordinary least squares regression examining the relationship between the percentage of public high schools with JROTC programs in each state and the percentage of the state's area that is made up of military bases, we did not find statistically significant relationships in our analyses. However, it is not clear whether these nonsignificant results indicate the lack of a relationship between JROTC units and the concentration of retirees or military units or the resolution of our indicators of these variables at the state level. More-nuanced analyses based on other measures of these variables might yield different inferences.

As noted, we were limited to a total of nine interviews with non-DoD employees because we could not obtain a PRA clearance. As a result, we only have a limited number of interviews directly from the school level. We supplemented the limited number of school interviews by talking to multiple JROTC regional directors, from all services, who are DoD employees and are therefore not subject to these PRA restrictions.

JROTC Unit Distribution, by State and Service

State	Percentage of JROTC Units in State Sponsored by Each Service (Including the District of Columbia)				Percentage of Public High Schools in State with JROTC Unit (Including the District of Columbia)
	Air Force	Army	Marine Corps	Navy	
AK	38	44	6	13	23
AL	16	72	5	8	27
AR	28	56	2	14	14
AZ	36	41	9	14	10
CA	30	38	9	23	9
CO	25	58	6	11	10
CT	31	38	8	23	5
DC	8	77	0	15	38
DE	44	31	6	19	44
FL	23	50	4	23	46
GA	28	47	6	19	56
HI	17	67	4	13	60
IA	25	50	25	0	2
ID	33	33	33	0	2
IL	18	57	7	17	10
IN	23	48	15	15	11

State	Percentage of JROTC Units in State Sponsored by Each Service (Including the District of Columbia)				Percentage of Public High Schools in State with JROTC Unit (Including the District of Columbia)
	Air Force	Army	Marine Corps	Navy	
KS	35	45	10	10	6
KY	17	65	6	13	23
LA	22	59	8	12	42
MA	30	35	22	14	11
MD	32	30	10	29	30
ME	25	63	0	13	6
MI	14	80	2	5	5
MN	45	27	9	18	1
MO	32	52	9	7	10
MS	21	62	4	13	27
MT	0	100	0	0	1
NC	30	52	4	13	49
ND	40	60	0	0	3
NE	36	57	0	7	5
NH	50	25	13	13	9
NJ	31	39	8	21	13
NM	17	41	20	22	20
NV	29	43	6	23	31
NY	22	41	11	26	5
OH	33	38	5	24	7
OK	35	45	8	13	9
OR	20	50	10	20	4
PA	37	44	11	9	8
RI	20	60	20	0	8

	Percentage of JROTC Units in State Sponsored by Each Service (Including the District of Columbia)				Percentage of Public High Schools in State with JROTC Unit (Including the District of Columbia)
State	Air Force	Army	Marine Corps	Navy	
SC	25	50	6	19	62
SD	14	71	14	0	4
TN	19	62	3	15	33
TX	26	50	7	17	24
UT	50	50	0	0	5
VA	24	44	8	23	35
VT	25	75	0	0	9
WA	35	27	8	30	7
WI	25	75	0	0	1
WV	25	63	6	6	26
WY	33	67	0	0	4

SOURCES: Project calculations from JROTC program data provided by the services in 2015 and the NCES Common Core of Data from the 2012–2013 school year.

Abbreviations

CSIS	Center for Strategic and International Studies
DoD	U.S. Department of Defense
GPA	grade point average
JROTC	Junior Reserve Officers' Training Corps
NCES	National Center for Education Statistics
NCO	noncommissioned officer
NDCC	National Defense Cadet Corps
PDT	Personal Development Test
PRA	Paperwork Reduction Act

References

Alper, Omer, Curtis Gilroy, Aline Quester, and Mark Rosen, *Assessing the Cost of Restructuring Army JROTC Instructor Pay*, Arlington, Va.: CNA, 2015.

Bachmann, John E., *The Effect of Participation or Non-Participation in a Junior Reserve Officers' Training Corps (JROTC) Program on Leadership Behavior and Self-Esteem Among JROTC and Non-JROTC High School Juniors*, dissertation, University of San Francisco, 1994.

Biggs, Carl Leon, *Junior Reserve Officers Training Corps: A Comparison of Achievement, High School Graduation, College Enrollment, and Military Enlistment Rates of High School Students in Missouri*, dissertation, University of Arkansas, 2010.

Bulach, Cletus R., "Comparison of Character Traits for JROTC Students Versus Non-JROTC Students," *Education*, Vol. 122, No. 3, 2002, pp. 559–563.

Cassel, R. N., and P. Chow, *The Personal Development Test (PDT)*, Chula Vista, Calif.: Project Innovation, 2001.

Center for Strategic and International Studies, *Junior Reserve Officers' Training Corps: Contributing to America's Communities*, Washington, D.C., 1999.

Code of Federal Regulations, Title 32, Section 542.7, Program Information, July 1, 2005.

Corbett, John W., and Arthur T. Coumbe, "JROTC: Recent Trends and Developments," *Military Review*, Vol. 8, No. 1, 2001, pp. 40–48.

Crawford, Alice M., Gail F. Thomas, and Armando X. Estrada, *Best Practices at Junior Reserve Officers' Training Corps Units*, Monterey, Calif.: Naval Post Graduate School, 2004.

CSIS—*See* Center for Strategic and International Studies.

Curran, Dennis D., *An Analysis of High School Junior ROTC and Its Effect on Student Achievement and Post-Secondary School Outcomes*, Monterey, Calif.: Naval Postgraduate School, 2007.

Days, Janet, and Yee Ling Ang, *An Empirical Examination of the Impact of JROTC Participation on Enlistment, Retention and Attrition*, Monterey, Calif.: Naval Postgraduate School, 2004.

Department of Defense Instruction 1205.13, *Junior Reserve Officers' Training Corps (JROTC) Program*, Washington, D.C.: U.S. Department of Defense, February 6, 2006.

Eisenhardt, K. M., "Building Theories from Case Study Research," *Academy of Management Review*, Vol. 14, No. 4, 1989, pp. 532–550.

Elliot, Marc N., Lawrence M. Hanser, and Curtis L. Gilroy, "Career Academies: Evidence of Positive Student Outcomes," *Journal of Education for Students Placed at Risk*, Vol. 7, No. 1, 2002, pp. 71–90.

Flowers, Chipman L., *Leadership, Self-Esteem, Average Daily Attendance, School Suspension: A Comparative Study of Army Junior Reserve Officers' Training Corps (JROTC) Sophomores and Non-JROTC Participating Sophomores*, Auburn, Ala.: Auburn University, 1999.

Grubb, D., J. Osborne, and D. Fasko, "Core Value: After Three Years of Research, What Do We Know?" paper presented at the annual meeting of the Mid-South Educational Research Association, New Orleans, La., November 1998.

Hanser, Lawrence M., and Abby E. Robyn, *Implementing High School JROTC Career Academies*, Santa Monica, Calif.: RAND Corporation, MR-741-OSD, 2000. As of March 24, 2017:
http://www.rand.org/pubs/monograph_reports/MR741.html

Hawkins, C. A., Jr., *An Analysis of Selected Learning Outcomes Involving Junior Reserve Officers' Training Corps (JROTC) Cadets and Non-JROTC Students*, dissertation, University of Virginia, 1988.

Kariuki, Patrick, and Linda Williams, "The Relationship Between Character Traits and Academic Performance of AFJROTC High School Students," paper presented at the Annual Conference of the Mid-South Educational Research Association, Birmingham, Ala., 2006.

Morris, Debra Sue, *North Carolina High School Principals: Perceptions of Junior Reserve Officer Training Corps (JROTC) Programs*, Charlotte: University of North Carolina, Charlotte, 2003.

National Center for Education Statistics, "Common Core of Data," web page, undated-a. As of April 18, 2017:
https://nces.ed.gov/ccd/pubschuniv.asp

———, "Identification of Rural Locales," web page, undated-b.

NCES—*See* National Center for Education Statistics.

Office of the Deputy Assistant Secretary of Defense, *2014 Demographics: Profile of the Military Community*, Washington, D.C., 2014. As of March 24, 2017:
http://download.militaryonesource.mil/12038/MOS/Reports/
2014-Demographics-Report.pdf

Office of the Deputy Under Secretary of Defense (Installations and Environment), *Base Structure Report: Fiscal Year 2010 Baseline; A Summary of DoD's Real Property Inventory*, Washington, D.C.: U.S. Department of Defense, 2010. As of April 18, 2017:
http://www.globalsecurity.org/military/library/report/2009/
090930_fy10_baseline_dod_bsr.pdf

Pema, Elda, and Stephen Mehay, "The Effect of High School JROTC on Student Achievement, Educational Attainment and Enlistment," *Southern Economic Journal*, Vol. 76, No. 4, 2009a.

———, "The Impact of the High School JROTC Program: Does Treatment Timing and Intensity Matter?" *Defence and Peace Economics*, Vol. 21, No. 3, 2009b, pp. 229–247.

———, *What Does Occupation-Related Vocational Education Do? Evidence from an Internal Labor Market*, Monterey, Calif.: Naval Postgraduate School, 2009c.

Perusse, Rachelle, *Perceptions of School Counselors Towards JROTC in Virginia Public Schools*, Richmond: Virginia Polytechnic Institute and State University, 1997.

Powell, Colin L., *My American Journey* New York: Random House, 1995.

Public Law 64-85, National Defense Act of 1916, June 3, 1916.

Public Law 88-647, Reserve Officers' Training Corps Vitalization Act of 1964, October 13, 1964.

Public Law 89-10, Elementary and Secondary Education Act of 1965, April 11, 1965.

Public Law 94-361, Department of Defense Appropriation Authorization Act of 1977, July 14, 1976.

Public Law 102-484, National Defense Authorization Act for Fiscal Year 1993, October 23, 1992.

Public Law 110-417, National Defense Authorization Act for Fiscal Year 2009, October 14, 2008.

Rivas, R. O., *Development of Self-Esteem and Learning Skills in Students Participating in the Army Junior Reserve Officers' Training Corps (JROTC)*, dissertation, Loyola University, 1995.

Roberts, W. E., *Leadership, Citizenship and Self-Reliance: A Comparison of Army Junior Reserve Officers' Training Corps (JROTC) High School Senior Cadets and Non-ROTC High School Seniors*, dissertation, University of San Francisco, 1991.

Schmidt, Raymond, "JROTC Cadets in Leadership Training Display Significantly Higher Personal Development Than Typical Students," *Education*, Vol. 122, No. 2, 2001, pp. 302–306.

————, "122 JROTC Students from 30 Different High Schools Out-do 766 Typical High School Students on Personal Development," *Education*, Vol. 123, No. 4, 2003, pp. 665–667.

Seiverling, R. F., *A Study to Measure the Effectiveness of Junior Reserve Officers' Training Corps (JROTC) Programs in Pennsylvania's Public Secondary Schools*, dissertation, Pennsylvania State University, 1973.

Senate Report 113-211, accompanying Department of Defense Appropriations Bill, 2015, 113th Congress, 2d session, July 17, 2014.

Stephanic, Kim K., *The Junior Reserve Officers' Training Corps (JROTC): A Review of the Literature*, Washington, D.C.: Office of Accession Policy, U.S. Department of Defense, 2010.

Stogdill, R. M., *Manual for the Leader Behavior Description Questionnaire—Form XII*, Columbus, Ohio: Bureau of Business Research, The Ohio State University, 1963.

Thorpe L. P., W. W. Clark, and E. W. Tiegs, *California Test of Personality*, Los Angeles: California Test Bureau, 1953.

United States Code, Title 10, Chapter 102, Junior Reserve Officers' Training Corps, Sections 2031–2034, January 3, 2012.

U.S. Army, "AJROTC FAQS," web page, undated. As of June 12, 2017: https://www.usarmyjrotc.com/JROTC_faq.html

U.S. Census Bureau, "R2101: Percent of the Civilian Population 18 Years and Over Who Are Veterans—United States—States; and Puerto Rico," 2014 American Community Survey, American FactFinder, 2014.

U.S. Census Bureau, "Geography: Geographic Terms and Concepts—Census Divisions and Census Regions," web page, February 9, 2015.

U.S. Department of Education, Institute of Education Sciences, and National Center for Education Statistics, *High School and Beyond, 1980: A Longitudinal Survey of Students in the United States*, Ann Arbor, Mich.: Inter-university Consortium for Political and Social Research, 2001.

U.S. Department of Education and National Center for Education Statistics, *National Education Longitudinal Study, 1988*, Chicago: National Opinion Research Center; Ann Arbor, Mich.: Inter-university Consortium for Political and Social Research, 1990.

Williams-Bonds, Carmen, *A Comparison of the Academic Achievement and Perceptions of Leadership Skills and Citizenship Traits of JROTC, Student Athletes, and Other Students in an Urban High School Setting*, dissertation, Lindenwood University, 2013.